JACK RUSSELL TERRIERS

KW 164S

Distributed by T.F.H. Publications, Inc.
Neptune City, NJ

JACK RUSSELL TERRIERS

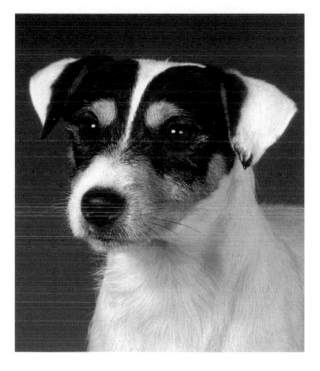

Anna Katherine Nicholas

T.F.H. Publications, Inc.
One TFH Plaza
Third and Union Avenues
Neptune City, NJ 07753

This book has been published with the intent to provide accurate and authoritative information in regard to the subject matter within. While every precaution has been taken in preparation of this book, the publisher and author assume no responsibility for errors or omissions. Neither is any liability assumed for damages resulting from the use of the information herein.

ISBN 0-7938-2379-X

Printed and bound in the United States of America

www.tfh.com

About This Book

Jack Russell Terriers is an updated version of the best-selling, breed-specific series from T. F. H. Publications. This modernized edition of the popular guide contains the most recent information available about the breed, from its history and origins to training techniques, as well as tips on selecting the right dog for you, grooming, feeding, obedience training, exercise, and health care. Complemented by all-new photographs, each book in the series provides purebred dog owners with all the advice they will need to raise a happy, healthy dog.

Other T.F.H. Books available on Jack Russell Terriers:

A New Owner's Guide to Jack Russell Terriers
Peggy Swagger & Linda Bollinger

The Guide to Owning a Jack Russell Terrier
George Kosloff

Contents

The Jack Russell Terrier was first bred in the south of England in the mid-1800s.

CHAPTER 1

Origin and History of the Jack Russell Terrier

The Jack Russell Terrier, or JR as he is affectionately called, is a sturdy little dog, a working terrier of a type created and developed by the Reverend John Russell, widely known as Parson Jack and frequently referred to as "The Sporting Parson."

Parson Jack was born in 1795. His father was a noted sportsman who took tremendous interest in hounds, terriers, and the working and hunting of both; and he was also a clergyman. His son can truly be said to have patterned his own life in the senior Russell's footsteps.

The Jack Russell Terrier is named for Reverend John Russell, a noted sportsman who was interested in hounds and terriers.

While attending Exeter College at Oxford, Jack's attention was caught one day by a small terrier riding past him on a milkwagon. He was so attracted to this little dog that he immediately wished to own her, and a deal was promptly made. This bitch was "Trump," who was to become a legend in Jack Russell history, figuring so strongly in JR pedigrees that she is said to have appeared in the background of every dog born during the next five decades.

Trump has been described as a bitch of excellent type and of a size approximating that of a vixen fox. Her complete whiteness was adorned only with a patch of dark tan over each eye and ear, with a similar penny-sized dot at the root of her tail. The thick, close coat was of a slightly wire-haired texture, but so close and dense as to provide the utmost protection for the wearer. The body impressed one by its obviously sturdy soundness; the legs by their straightness; and the feet by their perfection. This was clearly a bitch well equipped for the work of a terrier. Small wonder that she became one of Parson Jack's most treasured possessions!

If you ever take a trip to England, be sure to visit the Jack Russell Inn, which is located close to Barnstaple. On the sign identifying the inn, you will see a picture of Trump, which is a reproduction of the lovely portrait Parson Jack had made during the lifetime of his special favorite.

Parson Jack especially admired terriers that were pure white or carried only very slight marking. All of his dogs were apparently white or predominantly so. It must have aroused considerable comment when, feeling as he did on the subject, Parson Jack bred his beloved Trump to a terrier that was black and tan, probably of the old broken-coated type. Be that as it may, the results of this litter made their name in Jack Russell history, as two of the progeny became the foundation for this particular type of terrier.

Fox Terrier historians have written of the Reverend John Russell as "the world's oldest breeder of Fox Terriers," his years of activity having encompassed almost his entire lifetime from his youth until his death at 88 years of age. He had very definite ideas about terriers, including a strong dislike of what, in the beginning, were considered to be "show-type" terriers. In his own breeding program, emphasis was placed on the working qualities of his dogs, as exemplified by soundness, stamina, spirit, and the best conformation to enable the dog to last well on the trail and to "go to ground" with ease, should doing so become necessary.

There are those who believe that Parson Jack developed his dogs

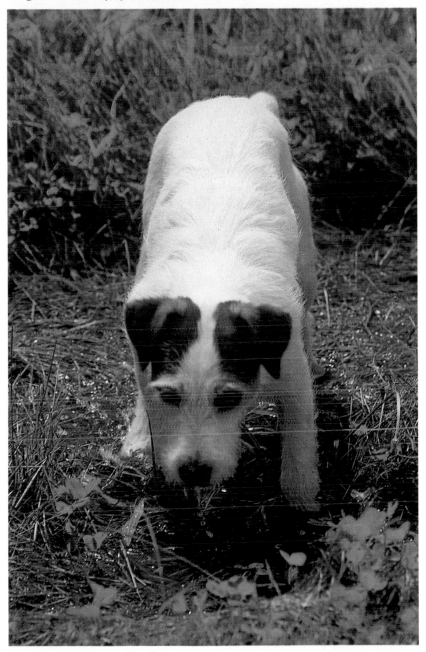

Despite his small size, the Jack Russell Terrier is a tough dog that is on his toes at all times.

entirely through the breeding of Trump descendants completely within their own family. There are others who claim that this is not the case and that the Parson had been quick to "buy in" any likely dog or bitch he saw that looked as though it would make a useful outcross for his dogs. Each school of thought has its followers, and who can say what the truth may be? It is known, however, that Parson Jack kept his own pedigree registry most carefully.

It is sensible to assume that, while using Trump as the mainstay of his breeding program, Parson Jack would have found it desirable to introduce an occasional outcross. Linebreeding is certainly excellent up to a point; but then the necessity arises of bringing in different breeding to correct a weakness, improve on some specific feature, or add a bit of new life to the strain. Reverend Russell had very definite ideas about his dogs and how he wanted them to look and to function. Bearing this in mind, one would think it unreasonable to believe that such heavy emphasis was placed on just one bitch as some have claimed. A bit of outcrossing would have served to strengthen rather than dilute the good qualities aimed for in these little terriers.

Very few breeds of dog carry the name of the individual who created them as a breed. Jack Russell is one; Herr Dobermann is another

Jack Russells are hardy, healthy dogs that live 12 to 14 years or more.

honored in this manner. Jack Russell performed a very real service for all who enjoy dogs. His time, effort, and thought led to the production of the appealing and delightful little terriers that bear his name.

It seems fairly obvious, the Parson having been a known breeder of Fox Terriers, that these are the dogs from which Jack Russells originally were bred, coming from specimens who pleased the Parson's eye. We have already mentioned his preference for white dogs. Another important feature to him was a fairly decent length of leg, which enabled the terriers to keep up more easily when running with the hounds. He also preferred to work only with wire-haired terriers, feeling that, in smooth-coated terriers, he might run up against a Bull Terrier cross, which would make for unsuitability to participate in the hunt, as it was not wanted nor expected that the terriers should hurt the foxes.

In 1862, England's first dog show took place, the famous Bath event at Exeter, which still remains one of the most prestigious in that country. Parson Jack was among the exhibitors at this opening show, winning a first prize with one of his dogs. The Parson also became a dog show judge of Fox Terriers, although his strict preference for working terriers bred specifically for that purpose remained. His judging assignments included the Biddeford show in 1863 and the famed Crystal Palace competition in 1874.

When the Kennel Club of Great Britain was organized in 1873, Reverend John Russell was among the earliest members, a founder who retained his membership throughout his lifetime. The Kennel Club Stud Book was issued in 1874, when the important task of drawing up bylaws and policies for the future began. These included a ruling that dogs exhibited at any dog show held under non-Kennel Club rules and regulations would be permanently disqualified by the Kennel Club; then, in 1880, it was proclaimed that any dog who was not registered with the Kennel Club could not be exhibited under Kennel Club rules.

Despite his Kennel Club membership, Reverend Russell upheld his independence in the matter of registration by continuing to keep his own pedigrees. In addition, he showed no interest in drawing up a breed standard for the Jack Russell Terrier, which would have been one of the first steps necessary had he contemplated admission to the Kennel Club Stud Book. This probably increased the speculation that perhaps Parson Jack was slipping in a likely looking purchase here and there. To this day, Jack Russell breeders are known to take the stand, in both England and the US, that they wish to avoid Kennel Club registration for their breed; they feel it is likely that the working qualities of terriers will degenerate with breed registration, leading to emphasis on producing show-type rather than working-type dogs. However, since 1990, the Kennel Club has recognized the Jack Russell Terrier under the name "Parson Jack Russell Terrier."

FURTHER DEVELOPMENT IN GREAT BRITAIN

The National (parent) Specialty club for Jack Russell Terriers in England is the Parson Jack Russell Terrier Club of Great Britain. Its duties include: overseeing the club government and enforcing the rules; upholding the constitution and bylaws; drawing up the breed standard; guarding the quality of the breed as described in that standard; and keeping an accurate, complete registry of all eligible Jack Russells in England.

Regional clubs are smaller organizations that operate within the boundaries of specified territory. There are regional clubs for Jack Russell Terriers to be found on the Isle of Wight, North Wales and South Wales, Thames Valley, Border Counties, Midlands, Southeast and Southwest. In addition to the regionals are clubs affiliated with the national. These include the Jack Russell Club of Australia, the Jack Russell Clubs of Belgium, South Africa, and the US, each with regional chapter clubs of their own.

Well-run regional clubs, offering a full program of Jack Russell-related activities, are of tremendous importance to the breed, providing the opportunity for fanciers within that area to become acquainted with others of similar interests and to share experiences and the pleasure brought by their dogs. As for the national club, in a breed where the entire control of activities lies within the realm of that club, every fancier active in the breed should know that membership in this group is a necessity.

The more closely allied one is with the clubs promoting and supporting the breed of interest to us, the more pleasure and satisfaction derived from them. You will be amazed how suddenly your spare time is filled to capacity with interesting activities revolving around your JRs, and your thirst for knowledge and desire to participate are satisfied.

CHAPTER 2

Jack Russell Terriers in the US

Without a doubt, the most significant day in the history of Jack Russell Terriers in the US was the one on which Mrs. Nelson Slater presented a JR puppy named "Rare" to her good friend Mrs. Harden Crawford III, of Hamilton Farm in Far Hills, New Jersey.

It was around 1960 when this event took place, and the results have been far-reaching, starting Ailsa Crawford off on a project that has created a whole new world of activity among Jack Russell Terrier owners in the US.

Jack Russell Terriers are noted for their high intelligence. This Jack Russell Terrier loves to play with his Nylabone® chew toys.

No gift could have been more successful than Rare. Mrs. Crawford was so enchanted by her JR puppy that she was eager to learn everything there was to know about the breed, to share this knowledge with others, and to protect in every way the natural quality and character that had so completely and quickly charmed her. In Mrs. Crawford's opinion (and that of all who have become acquainted with Jack Russells), these dogs are truly special.

No important JR kennel in England was overlooked as Mrs. Crawford made the rounds. She made friends there with JR authorities, including Joan Begbie, who helped immeasurably. She became Ailsa Crawford's good friend and mentor. Mrs. Crawford admired the quality of Miss Sexton's Breach Hills, that of Farm Fir Hill, Eastleigh Kennels, and the others at which she was warmly welcomed. When she returned home, Mrs. Crawford had made some splendid selections on which to found her Hamilton Farm Jack Russell Terriers.

Mrs. Crawford owned a busy, large, and influential kennel of JRs over the years between the acquisition of Rare and 1978. Her dogs were known and owned around the world, having served as "trail blazers" for many new kennels and fanciers. All of this involved a great deal of work, to the extent of being a full-time job. Yet along with this responsibility, Mrs. Crawford founded the Jack Russell Terrier Club of America (JRTCA), became its president, and took on the job of handling the registry of Jack Russells in the US. To do all this was an awesome task, even for someone as energetic and devoted to the breed as Mrs. Crawford. And so it was that in 1978, Mrs. Crawford realized that she could not continue with the full responsibility for so many things. Thus it was that Hamilton Farm Jack Russells were signed over to the kennel manager who had done such a good job through the years, and Mrs. Crawford settled down to concentrate on the registry and on the club. Mrs. Crawford herself enjoys membership in the Jack Russell Terrier Club of Great Britain, the Jack Russell Terrier Club of Australia, and the Jack Russell Terrier Club of South Africa, in addition to the US club. She has made trips to England at least once annually during the past several decades, most of them for reasons involving JRs. She has judged and worked terriers in both England and the US.

The rapidly rising popularity of Jack Russells is, we know, a matter of concern to the people who are anxious to see the breed retain its sporting and working qualities and to establish a definite type. Not too many years ago, there were only a few hundred JRs included in the

Her small stature and adorable appearance make the Jack Russell Terrier a favorite among dog fanciers.

Jack Russell Terriers develop with good speed and generally mature mentally before their first birthday.

registry of the JRTCA. By now, the number must exceed several thousand, and it still continues to grow. In order to protect the true Jack Russell, only dogs belonging to members of the club are eligible for favorable action and entry in the registry. Information regarding parentage and bloodlines of the dog must be provided along with a photograph (from which its adherence to correct type can be ascertained), whenever an application for inclusion in the registry is received. It is interesting to note that although hundreds of applications are approved each year for entry in the registry, about an equal number are returned as being unsuitable.

Both the British and the US Jack Russell registries are run on the same principles. Both maintain a complete record of the bloodlines and locations of dogs considered acceptable for stud, and both willingly make suggestions as to the best possibility for use on a particular bitch. In addition, both keep a current list of puppies available for sale as pets or for breeding purposes.

If you are new in Jack Russells and are anxious to raise stock considered suitable for the registry, be sure to keep in mind that one can only become a recognized breeder by limiting one's Jack Russell breeding to terriers that are listed in the registry. Another service of the JRTCA is the offer of advertising space to members in the organization's quarterly newsletter.

The principal aim of the JRTCA is to protect and preserve the courage, stamina, and intelligence for which these little terriers have been created and raised. Complete mental and physical soundness takes precedence over all other qualities. The club especially fears inbreeding, which is one of the reasons that the majority of dedicated JR fanciers like the system the way it is, with the club keeping its own registry rather than having the breed under the jurisdiction of any other club. However, in 1985, breeders who did not agree with this philosophy formed a new club called the Jack Russell Terrier Breeders Association, now known as the Jack Russell Terrier Association of America (JRTAA). The JRTAA applied for American Kennel Club (AKC) recognition and received it in 1997. The JRTCA continues to adamantly oppose this affiliation.

Do not for one moment think that Jack Russells that are registered with the JRTCA are lacking in competitive activities. This is definitely not the case. Working terrier trials are frequent, and clubs affiliated with the JRTCA sponsor Jack Russell Terrier Trials, under its sanction, almost on a weekly basis somewhere in the US. These trials are similar to those in Great Britain. The principal highlight on the calendar is the National Specialty.

The formats for these events are divided into three categories. First come the conformation classes, with a trophy and six ribbons awarded in each. Classification is divided by size: Jack Russells 10 to 12 inches tall at the withers; Jack Russells 12 to 15 inches; and by sex. The classes are for puppies six to twelve months of age, for JRs over

These cute Jack Russell Terrier pups will be your best friends if taken care of properly.

one year of age, and for puppies four to six months old; these are divided by sex if enough dogs are entered.

A Puppy Conformation Champion and Reserve are offered, judged between first and second prize winners in the four classes for puppies ranging between six months and one year of age. Best Dog, Bitch, and Reserve are judged between the Open Class first prize winners in the two size divisions. Conformation Champion and Reserve are then judged between the winners of those awards.

There are also regional titles to be competed for and won. For example, Wyndhaven Farm, Saratoga Jack Russell Terrier Club, Goldens Bridge Jack Russell Club and the Greater New York Jack Russell Terrier Club offer special "New York Bred Classes" at these four JR trials, the winners of which are awarded points. The dog or bitch winning the highest number of points is presented with an award as "Best New York Bred Jack Russell" for that year, presentation being made at the National in October.

There are Miscellaneous Classes judged on conformation; classes for children who are handlers; Pairs Classes and Family Classes (these comparable to Brace Class and Stud Dog or Brood Bitch at AKC shows). There is also a conformation award for Working Terrier, judged on the breed standard.

Go-to-Ground Classes are very exciting. Novice and Open are provided for Jack Russells who are six months or older, and competition for the Championship Working Certificate is the big excitement of the day. The winner of this class, who must previously have gained a Trial Certificate or an American Working Terrier Certificate, thus becomes a Go-to-Ground Champion.

Jack Russell racing brings with it great excitement and, we feel sure, a bit of betting. There are flat races, steeplechase races (over hurdles not more than 8 inches high) and higher hurdle races (over 8 inches). The grand climax is reached with the stakes races, entered only by post entry. So, you see, there is plenty of competitive fun to be had with your Jack Russell!

There is no doubt but that interest in and enthusiasm for Jack Russell Terriers is growing constantly in the US.

CHAPTER 3

A Description of the Jack Russell Terrier

Jack Russell Terriers are many sorts of dog to many people. We have already discussed the breed's sporting and working qualities, pointing out the usefulness of these dogs in hunting foxes with the sportsmen who enjoy this activity. Jack Russells also perform the more prosaic job of keeping the premises free of rodents with impressive efficiency—at farms, kennels, or stables. They are true terriers, from whisker to tail, in every sense of the word.

Not all of us, however, love chasing over the countryside behind a fox or own large country properties in need of a rodent eliminator. What, then, about those of us who just need an all-around family dog that will be fun to own, intelligent, and fit nicely into the household?

Breed standards vary from country to country and from registry to registry. Become familiar with the standard that applies to your area.

Jack Russells love to play with children. They also make keen, alert watchdogs.

It would be impossible, I assure you, to improve on a Jack Russell for any of those purposes. Game and hardy as they are, they also possess a keen appreciation of comfort; they bask in being permitted to share the household with their people and even with several other dogs (not just of their own breed), plus a cat or two. How well this works depends largely upon the tact displayed by the owner, seeing that all introductions to other animals with whom the home will be shared are handled tactfully, to assure good, jealousy-free future relations. This is true of pets no matter what the type or breed.

The keen intelligence of Jack Russells always makes them interesting to have around. Their delightful ways with people, their affection for their owner (and their eagerness for making this clear), and their obvious comfort in sharing your chair, sofa, or bed, or curling up on your lap as you read or watch television, make them ideal, no matter what your lifestyle.

Being small, Jack Russells are truly a most convenient size for taking with you on your travels, and they have the ability to settle in happily in an apartment, a house in the suburbs, or in the country. Their size makes a tremendous amount of exercise unnecessary, although they do seem practically tireless in the field, romping and playing or accompanying you on walks. You will find them conversation pieces in the city, as many people are unfamiliar with the breed and will stop you to inquire about that "adorable little dog." Many people also are likely to regard them as status symbols, owing to the number of prominent socialites and sportsmen who have already discovered their charm.

A dog this size is a convenience in small quarters, since they do make out well on a program of being walked at least a couple of times daily, with short potty breaks in between.

You may find JR puppies a bit inclined to chew; so before anything is damaged, try to head off this problem by providing a nice assortment of chew toys for your puppy's amusement. Do not leave a JR puppy alone, however, with an invitingly fringed Oriental rug or some other goody until you are sure that the destructive puppy stage has passed, as it almost certainly will with maturity.

Jack Russells adore playing with children. They also are very keen, alert watchdogs that seem to hear and know everything unusual that occurs and do not hesitate to announce the fact. Noise is a particular enemy of prowlers or burglars, and a Jack Russell on the premises will generally send those who are up to no good on their way.

The ideal Jack Russell stands between 12 and 14 inches in height at the withers. Weight should be between 13 and 17 pounds.

Of course, a dog as intelligent as the JR can be an instant success in obedience. Join such a class with your puppy, and he might soon be among the best obedience dogs in your area.

There are various types of competition in which JRs are eligible to compete. Make it a habit to attend some of the Jack Russell shows (and American Working Terrier Association Trials) in your area. These are really fun occasions, with lots to see and people with whom to exchange ideas about the breed.

PHYSICAL CHARACTERISTICS

The Jack Russell Terrier has been known in Great Britain for more than a century. Throughout this time, various changes have taken place in the physical characteristics of these little dogs. One of the chief differences between the JRTCA and the AKC standards as they exist today is in the accepted size of the breed.

The JRTCA Standard for the Jack Russell Terrier

In general appearance, the JR is a sturdy terrier, known for fearlessness and happy disposition; it has an alert air of supreme confidence. This is a tough (despite being small) dog that is on its toes at all times. The JR should measure, in the words of the standard,

The head should be strong and in proportion to the rest of the body.

between 10 and 15 inches at the withers, continuing that "the body length must be in proportion to the height and it should present a compact, balanced image, always being in solid, hard condition."

Under "Body," the standard points out that the chest should be shallow, narrow, and with "front legs set not too widely apart; thus creating an athletic look rather than too heavy and chesty an appearance." Suggested as a guide is that the chest should be sufficiently small to be easily spanned behind the shoulders by average-sized hands when the terrier is in fit, working condition. The feeling is that a dog so built

A Description of the Jack Russell Terrier

The rough-coated Jack Russell is double coated with a dense undercoat and a coarse wirelike top coat.

will thus be able to "go to ground" more easily than one with a fuller chest development. The back should be strong and straight, giving a balanced image as compared to the height of the terrier. There is a slight arching at the loin.

A well-balanced head should be well proportioned to the body. The skull is of moderate width at the ears, narrowing to the eyes; top skull flat. Stop is defined but not overly pronounced. Length of muzzle from nose to stop is slightly shorter than the distance from stop to occiput. Jaw is powerful and well boned with strongly muscled cheeks.

The almond-shaped eyes are dark in color and full of life and intelligence. Small "V"-shaped dropped ears of moderate thickness are carried forward close to the head. Teeth are strong, meeting in a scissors bite, i.e., inside tips of the upper teeth just slightly overlapping the outside tips of the lowers. The neck is clean, muscular, and of good length, widening gradually at the shoulder, which should be sloping and well laid back, fine at points and clearly cut at the withers.

Forelegs should be strong and straight boned, with joints in correct alignment. Elbows hang perpendicular to the body and work free of the sides. Strong, muscular hindquarters should be well put together with good angulation and bend at stifle, giving plenty of drive and propulsion from behind. Viewed from the rear, hocks must be straight. Round, firmly padded, catlike feet turn neither in nor out. The tail is set rather high, carried gaily, and is in proportion to body length. It should be about four inches long, providing a good hand hold.

Jack Russell coats are smooth without being sparse, as it is essential that they provide a certain amount of protection from the elements and undergrowth. Rough-coated JRs have a rough or broken coat that must never be woolly. White is the basic color and predominates with tan, black, or brown markings. Brindle markings are unacceptable. Movement is free, lively, and well coordinated, with straight action both in front and behind.

The JRTCA standard makes the following addenda. For showing purposes, JRs are classified in two categories: 10 to 12 1/2 inches, and over 12 1/2 up to 15 inches. The Jack Russell standard makes it clearly understood that old scars or injuries, the result of work or accident, should not be penalized, nor allowed to prejudice a JR's chances in the show ring, unless they interfere with its movement or with its ability to work, or utility at stud. Male animals should have two apparently normal testicles fully descended into the scrotum.

Faults to be penalized in Jack Russells in show competition include shyness or disinterest, over-aggressiveness, defects in bite, weak jaws, fleshy ears, down at shoulders, barrel ribs, out at elbows, narrow hips, straight stifles, weak feet, sluggish or unsound movement, dishing, plaiting, toeing, silky or woolly coats, shrill or weak voice, lack of muscle tone or skin tone, lack of stamina or lung reserve, and evidence of foreign blood.

It has been only within the past decade, following considerable discussion on both sides of the Atlantic, that the above description or standard for the breed was decided upon. One of the areas where considerable difference in the type of the dogs is concerned centers, of course, around the wide size range. Five inches is a considerable amount of leeway for this small a dog. It is, therefore, to be expected that the dogs that are only 10 inches in height or thereabouts have a lower set and longer bodied appearance than do those that are a couple of inches taller and are thus longer legged.

The American Kennel Club Standard for the Jack Russell Terrier

GENERAL APPEARANCE—The Jack Russell Terrier was developed in the south of England in the 1800's as a white terrier to work

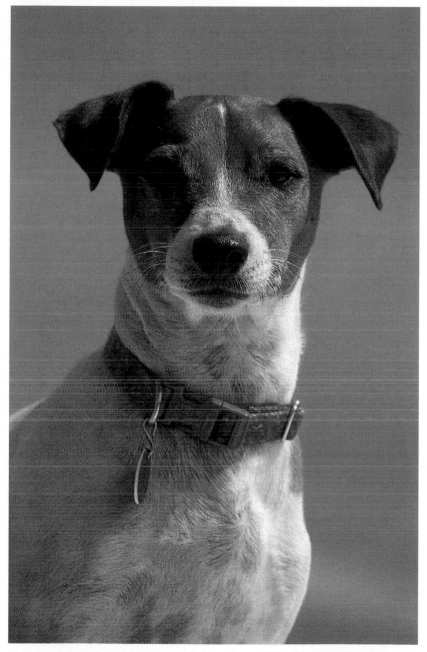

The eyes of the Jack Russell Terrier are dark in color and full of life and intelligence.

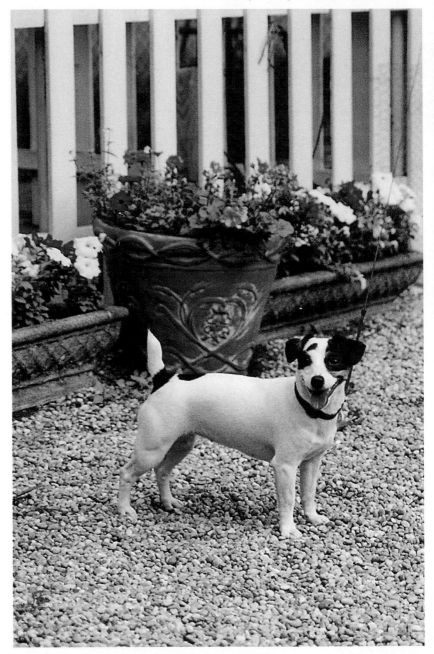

The Jack Russell's tail is strong, set high, and carried gaily.

The Jack Russell is an elegant, sprightly little terrier that is well balanced and well structured.

European red fox both above and below ground. The terrier was named for the Reverend John Russell, whose terriers trailed hounds and bolted foxes from dens so the hunt could ride on.

To function as a working terrier, he must possess certain characteristics: a ready attitude, alert and confident; balance in height and length; medium in size and bone, suggesting strength and endurance. Important to breed type is a natural appearance: harsh, weatherproof coat with a compact construction and clean silhouette. The coat is broken or smooth. He has a small, flexible chest to enable him to pursue his quarry underground and sufficient length of leg to follow the hounds. Old scars and injuries, the result of honorable work or accident, should not be allowed to prejudice a terrier's chance in the show ring, unless they interfere with movement or utility for work or breeding.

SIZE, PROPORTION, SUBSTANCE—*Size*—Both sexes are properly balanced between 12″ and 14″ at the withers. The ideal height of a mature dog is 14″ at the withers, and bitches 13″. Terriers whose heights measure either slightly larger or smaller than the ideal are not to be penalized in the show ring provided other points of their conformation, especially balance and chest span, are consistent with the breed standard. The weight of a terrier in hard working condition is usually between 13 - 17 lbs. *Proportion*—Balance is the keystone of the terrier's anatomy. The chief points of consideration are the relative proportions of skull and foreface, head and frame, height at withers and length of body. The height at withers is slightly greater than the distance from withers to tail, i.e. by possibly 1 to 1fi inches on a 14 inch dog. The measurement will vary according to height, the ratio of height to back being approximately 6:5.

Substance—The terrier is of medium bone, not so heavy as to appear coarse or so light as to appear racy. The conformation of the whole frame is indicative of strength and endurance.

Disqualification—Height under 12" or over 15".

HEAD—*Head*—Strong and in good proportion to the rest of the body, so the appearance of balance is maintained. *Expression*—Keen, direct, full of life and intelligence. *Eyes*—Almond shaped, dark in color, moderate in size, not protruding. Dark rims are desirable. *Ears*—Button ear. Small "V" shaped drop ears of moderate thickness carried forward close to the head with the tip so as to cover the orifice and pointing toward the eye. Fold is level with the top of the skull or slightly above. When alert, ear tips do not extend below the corner of the eye. *Skull*—Flat and fairly broad between the ears, narrowing slightly to the eyes. The stop is well defined but not prominent. *Muzzle*—Length from nose to stop is slightly shorter than the distance from stop to occiput. *Jaws*—Upper and lower are of fair and punishing strength. *Nose*—Must be black and fully pigmented. *Bite*—Teeth are large with complete dentition in a perfect scissors bite, i.e., upper teeth closely overlapping the lower teeth and teeth set square to the jaws. *Faults*—Light or yellow eye, round eye. Hound ear, fleshy ear, rounded tips. Level bite, missing teeth.

Disqualifications—Prick ears. Liver color nose. Four or more missing teeth. Overshot, under-shot or wry mouth.

NECK, TOPLINE, BODY—*Neck*—Clean and muscular, moderately arched, of fair length, gradually widening so as to blend well into the shoulders. *Topline*—Strong, straight, and level in motion, the loin slightly arched. *Body*—in overall length to height proportion, the dog appears approximately square and balanced. The back is neither short nor long. The back gives no appearance of slackness but is laterally flexible, so that he may turn around in an earth. Tuck-up is moderate. *Chest*—Narrow and of moderate depth, giving and athletic rather than heavily-chested appearance; must be flexible and compressible. The ribs are fairly well sprung, oval rather than round, not extending past the level of the elbow. *Tail*—Set high, strong, carried gaily but not over the back or curled. Docked so the tip is

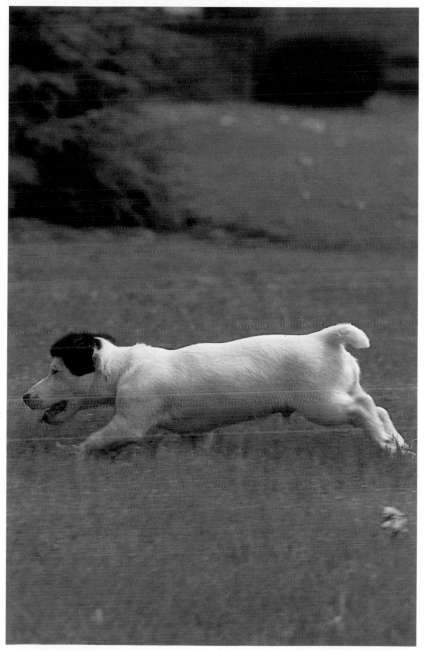

The Jack Russell Terrier's movement should be free, lively, and well coordinated, with straight action in front and behind.

approximately level to the skull, providing a good handhold. *Faults*—Chest not spannable or shallow; barrel ribs. Tail set low or carried over the back, i.e., squirrel tail.

FOREQUARTERS—*Shoulders*—Long and sloping, well laid back, cleanly cut at the withers. Point of shoulder sits in a plane behind the point of the prosternum. The shoulder blade and upper arm are of approximately the same length; forelegs are placed well under the dog. *Elbows*—hang perpendicular to the body, working free of the sides. Legs are strong and straight with good bone. Joints turn neither in nor out. *Pasterns*—firm and nearly straight. *Feet*—Round, cat-like, very compact, the pads thick and tough, the toes moderately arched pointing forward, turned neither in nor out. *Fault*—Hare feet.

HINDQUARTERS—Strong and muscular, smoothly molded, with good angulation and bend of stifle. Hocks near the ground, parallel, and driving in action. Feet as in front.

COAT—*Smooth*—Double-coated. Coarse and weatherproof. Flat but hard, dense and abundant, belly and undersides of thighs are not bare. *Broken*—Double-coated. Coarse and weatherproof. Short, dense undercoat covered with a harsh, straight, tight jacket which lies flat and close to the body and legs. There is a clear outline with

These Jack Russell Terriers display the playful, friendly temperament that is called for in the breed standard.

only a hint of eyebrows and beard. Belly and undersides of thighs are not bare. Coat does not show a strong tendency to curl or wave. *No sculpted furnishings. The terrier is shown in his natural appearance not excessively groomed. Sculpturing is to be severely penalized. Faults*—Soft, silky, wooly, or curly topcoat. Lacking undercoat.

COLOR—White, white with black or tan markings, or a combination of these, tri-color. Colors are clear. Markings are preferably confined to the head and root of tail. Heavy body markings are not desirable. Grizzle is acceptable and should not be confused with brindle. *Disqualification—Brindle markings.*

GAIT—Movement or action is the crucial test of conformation. The terrier's movement is free, lively, well coordinated, with straight action in front and behind. There should be ample reach and drive with a good length of stride.

TEMPERAMENT—Bold and friendly. Athletic and clever. At work he is a game hunter, tenacious and courageous. At home he is playful, exuberant and overwhelmingly affectionate. He is an independent and energetic terrier and requires his due portion of attention.

He should not be quarrelsome. Shyness should not be confused with submissiveness. Submissiveness is not a fault. *Sparring is not acceptable. Fault*—Shyness. *Disqualification—Overt aggression towards another dog or human.*

SPANNING—To measure a terrier's chest, span from behind, raising only the front feet from the ground, and compress gently. Directly behind the elbows is the smaller, firm part of the chest. The central part is usually larger but should feel rather elastic. Span with hands tightly behind the elbows on the forward portion of the chest. The chest must be easily spanned by average size hands. Thumbs should meet at the spine and fingers should meet under the chest. *This is a significant factor and a critical part of the judging process. The dog can not be correctly judged without this procedure.*

DISQUALIFICATIONS

Height under 12" or over 15". Prick ears, liver nose. Four or more missing teeth. Overshot, undershot or wry mouth. Brindle markings. Overt aggression towards other dogs or humans.

Approved: July 7, 1997
Effective: January 1, 1998

CHAPTER 4

Grooming the Jack Russell Terrier

In order to keep your dog looking good, you need to have the right tools. There is a large selection of grooming equipment available for every coat type, but there are some universal tools that every owner should have in order to perform general grooming duties.

Here is a list of grooming tools that every dog owner should have:

1. Slicker brush: This versatile brush can work on many different types of coat. The wire bristles grasp and remove a dog's undercoat, help reduce shedding, and keep the coat from becoming matted.

2. Flea comb: A fine-toothed flea comb will be helpful in getting hard-to-reach spots and will remove any flea or flea dirt that may be in your dog's coat.

3. Towels: Old towels are always handy and can be used to wipe off muddy paws and dry off wet coats.

4. Grooming glove: This tool (also called a hound glove) is wonderful for dogs with short coats because it helps loosen any dead hair and gets rid of surface dirt.

5. Nail clippers: Every dog, no matter what coat type, needs to have his nails trimmed. A good pair of canine nail clippers will be very useful if you decide to tackle this task yourself.

6. Doggy toothbrush and toothpaste: Keeping your puppy's teeth clean is essential for maintaining his good health. Be sure to purchase toothpaste and toothbrushes that are especially made for dogs. Never use human toothpaste when brushing your puppy's teeth. Dogs will not spit out the toothpaste, like humans do, but will swallow it, which can cause stomach upset and digestive problems. Also, the minty taste that humans enjoy probably will not be as appealing to your puppy as it is to you. Canine toothpaste comes in "doggy-friendly" flavors, such as beef and poultry, and is edible.

Grooming sessions should begin when your Jack Russell Terrier is still a pup. By beginning while he is young, he will become accustomed to the routine and enjoy being groomed.

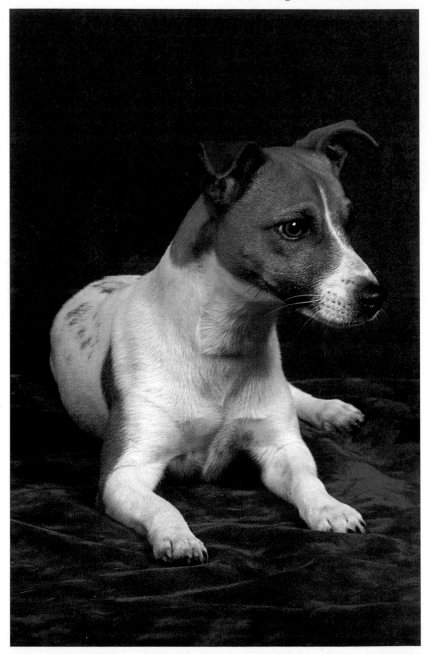

If you are uncomfortable with grooming your Jack Russell Terrier, there are professional groomers that can help.

7. Shampoo: There are many brands of canine shampoo available, as well as ones that have special purposes, such as flea shampoos, medicated shampoos, and whiteners. If you are unsure about what brand to buy, ask your veterinarian for a recommendation.

8. Conditioner: Dogs with long coats may need a conditioner to help remove tangles after bathing. As with shampoos, your vet can recommend a brand that is right for your dog.

9. Scissors: Blunt-nosed scissors are handy for trimming the excess fur on your dog's feet, legs, tail, or anal region, as well as for trimming your dog's whiskers.

GETTING STARTED

Puppyhood is the best time to start grooming procedures, because your dog will more easily become used to the grooming routine and soon come to expect it as part of his everyday life. This is especially true if you have a dog that requires extensive grooming or if you plan to show your puppy when he gets older. It is best to start out slowly so that he doesn't become overwhelmed or frightened, and then build on grooming time until you have the whole routine down pat.

If your puppy requires lots of grooming time, it is best to invest in a good grooming table. While he is getting beautiful, your dog's leash can be attached to the grooming arm on the table, which will help keep him secure. Most tables also have nonskid pads on the surface to keep your dog from sliding around. A grooming table will save

Jack Russell Terriers should be thoroughly brushed at least twice a week. Always brush the coat in the direction that it naturally lies.

Proper grooming can help keep your Jack Russell Terrier healthy. Daily brushing will allow you to inspect the dog's coat for fleas, ticks, and other parasites.

your back as well, because it can be adjusted to your height and make it unnecessary for you to bend over or kneel down.

Introduce your puppy to the grooming table slowly. Place him on it without doing anything to him, and give him a treat when you let him down. After you do this a several times, your puppy should eagerly get up on the grooming table. You can then start lightly brushing him and running any appliances like hair dryers or clippers before actually doing anything major to his coat. When he seems totally comfortable, you can start grooming him on a regular basis. This gradual introduction will ensure that your puppy grows to enjoy his grooming time with you. Once your puppy is accustomed to being touched, patted, and fussed over, you can start a grooming routine that will keep him looking clean and healthy.

NAIL CARE

Many dogs that run on gravel or pavement keep their toenails worn down, so they seldom need clipping. However, a dog that does-n't do much running or runs on grass will grow long toenails that can

Grooming the Jack Russell Terrier

All dogs need to have their nails trimmed from time to time. Use a clipper or a grinder to trim the nail to an appropriate length.

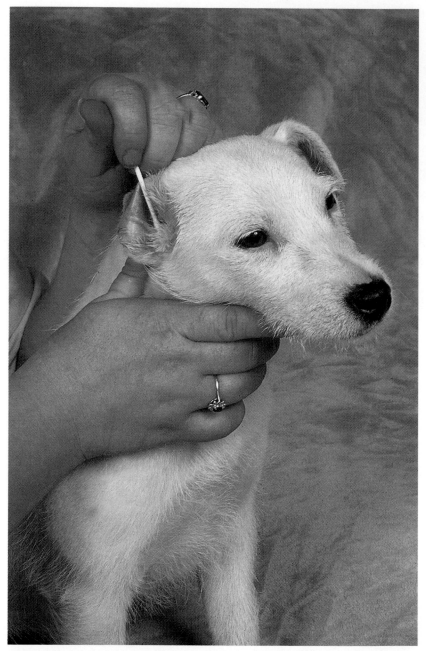

Your Jack Russell Terrier's ears need to be kept clean at all times. Wipe the ears with a soft, damp cloth or cotton swab to remove any dirt.

Trimming the hair away from your Jack Russell Terrier's ears will help prevent excessive wax buildup.

be harmful. Long nails will force the dog's toes into the air and spread his feet wide. In addition, the nails may force the dog into an unnatural stance that can produce lameness.

You can control your dog's toenails by cutting them with a special dog clipper or by filing them. Many dogs object to the clipping, and it takes some experience to learn just how to do it without cutting into the blood vessels (the quick). Your vet will probably examine your dog's nails whenever you bring him in and may trim them for you. He can show you how to do it yourself in the future. If you prefer, you can file the points off of your dog's nails every few weeks with a flat wooden file. Draw the file in only one direction—from the top of the nail downward, in a round stroke to the end of the nail or underneath. You'll need considerable pressure for the first few strokes to break through the hard surface, but then it gets easier. You may also use an electric nail grinder, but make sure you accustom the dog to the noise it makes first.

Incidentally, it's a good idea to keep your young puppy from walking on waxed or slippery floors, as this tends to break down the pasterns.

EAR CARE

Do not neglect your puppy's ears when going through your grooming steps, because it is very important to his health. Ear infections can be caused by excessive dirt, moisture, and bacteria accumulating in the ear canal. When taking care of your dog's ears, the first thing you should do is pluck or trim (with blunt-nosed scissors) the excess hair out. To keep them clean, use a cotton ball or washcloth dampened with commercial ear cleaner or mineral oil and wipe the inside of the earflap. If your puppy's ear is sore, has excess wax, or has a bad smell, he probably has an ear infection and needs to see the veterinarian immediately.

Never stick anything into your puppy's ear canal. When cleaning, wipe the outside area of the earflap only, or you may damage your dog's eardrum.

EYE CARE

It is fairly easy to keep your puppy's eyes clear, sparkling, and bright. First, make sure that you keep all debris (including hair) out of his eyes. Wipe your dog's eyes on a regular basis with a cotton ball or washcloth dipped in warm water. If your puppy's eyes appear red, cloudy, or swollen, or have excess tearing, contact your veterinarian.

Allowing your dog to play with a Nylafloss® will help to control plaque buildup.

Your Jack Russell Terrier needs to have his teeth checked regularly. If you notice plaque buildup, contact your veterinarian to have his teeth cleaned.

DENTAL CARE

Puppies need to chew. Chewing is an essential part of their physical and mental development, so you need to take good care of their teeth from the very beginning.

If you do not brush your dog's teeth on a regular basis, plaque builds up on the teeth and under the gums. If this plaque is not removed, periodontal disease, which is a bacterial infection, can occur. If left untreated, the bacteria can enter the bloodstream and spread to your puppy's vital organs. Other problems can develop as well, such as mouth abscesses and tooth loss. Also, puppies that don't receive good dental care can suffer from bad breath, a feature that does not endear them to humans or elicit doggy kisses.

It is much easier to brush your dog's teeth than you may think, as long as you have the right supplies. You should purchase a dog toothbrush or a finger toothbrush (a rubber cap that fits over your index finger) and toothpaste made for dogs. Start by accustoming your puppy to having your fingers in his mouth without brushing his teeth. When you are giving him his daily once-over, be sure to look in his mouth, exposing his gums and touching his teeth. Soon this will become just another part of his grooming routine.

Once he is used to this procedure, put some doggy-flavored toothpaste on the toothbrush and gently rub a few teeth at a time. Be sure to brush the teeth at the gum line. Use a circular motion when brushing and slowly make your way around your dog's upper teeth. Make sure to get the teeth in the back of the mouth, because these are the ones most prone to periodontal disease. When you are finished with the top, do the bottom in the same manner.

Daily brushing would be ideal, but try to do it at least four times a week. This will ensure that your puppy keeps his teeth healthy and keeps them for a long time.

CHAPTER 5

Selecting Your Dog

Now that you have decided which breed of dog suits your needs, your lifestyle, and your temperament, there will be much to consider before you make your final purchase. Getting a puppy on impulse may only cause heartbreak later; it makes much more sense to put some real thought into your canine investment, especially because it is likely that he will share many happy years with you.

Once you've mulled over the pluses and minuses of dog ownership, ask yourself a few questions concerning your needs and preferences for a dog. Read all that you can about your particular breed,

Jack Russell Terrier puppies are absolutely adorable. Take your time and examine a number of pups before making your final selection.

When visiting a breeder, her Jack Russell Terriers should look healthy and loved. They should not shy away from people.

and visit a few dog shows. At the shows you will be surrounded by people who can give you all the details about the breed in which you are interested. Decide if you want a household pet or a show dog. Would you prefer a male or female? Puppy or adult?

If you buy from a breeder, ask to visit the premises and if possible, see the puppy's parents and other relatives. These breeders are always willing to discuss any breed problems and how they should be dealt with. This is also a good time to ask him to help you with your decision. When you have settled on the dog you want, discuss with the seller the dog's temperament, the animal's positive and negative aspects, any health problems he might have, his feeding and grooming requirements, and whether or not the dog has been immunized. Reputable sellers will be willing to answer any questions you might have that pertain to the dog you have selected, and often they will make themselves available if you call for advice or if you encounter problems after you've made your purchase.

Most breeders and sellers want to see their dogs placed in loving, responsible homes, so they are careful about who buys their animals. As the dog's new owner, prepare yourself to answer some questions from the breeder.

Selecting the right Jack Russell Terrier should not be a quick decision. Remember that this dog will be living with you for many years to come.

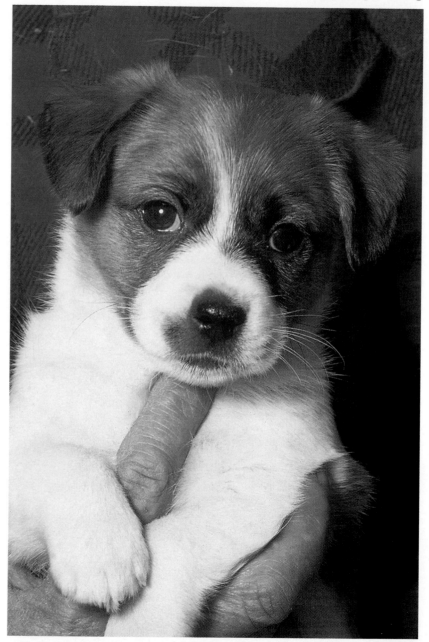

Make sure you buy your Jack Russell Terrier pup from a reputable breeder. If you are not comfortable with a particular breeder or the way the puppies are handled or kept, visit another breeder.

Selecting Your Dog

WHERE TO BUY

You can choose among several places to buy your dog. One source is a kennel whose business is breeding show-quality dogs; such kennels may have extra pups for sale. Another source is the one-dog owner who wants to sell the puppies from an occasional litter to pay the expenses of his small-scale breeding operation. To find such kennels and part-time breeders and hobbyists, check the classified section of your local newspaper or look in your telephone directory. Whichever source you choose, you can usually tell in a very short time whether or not the puppies will make healthy and happy pets. If they are clean, plump, and lively, they are probably in good health. Sometimes you will have the advantage of seeing the puppies' dam and perhaps their sire and other relatives. Remember that the mother, having just raised a demanding family, may not be looking her best; but if she is sturdy, friendly, and well-mannered, her puppies should be too.

If you feel that something is lacking in the care or condition of the dogs, it is better to look elsewhere than to buy hastily and regret it afterward. Buy a healthy dog with a good disposition, one that has been properly socialized and likes being around people.

Before you select a Jack Russell Terrier, you need to decide whether you want a pet- or show-quality dog.

A reputable breeder wants to see her pups go to loving, respectable homes and will ask you many questions to ensure the well-being of her Jack Russell Terriers.

If you cannot find a local breeder, write to the secretary of the national breed club or kennel club and a reputable one will be recommended to you. Puppies are sometimes shipped to other states by reputable breeders. In these instances, pictures and pedigree information are usually sent beforehand to help you decide. Many breed clubs provide a puppy referral service, so you may want to look into this before making your final decision.

PET OR SHOW DOG

Conscientious breeders strive to maintain desirable qualities in their breeds. At the same time, they are always working to improve on what they have already achieved, and they do this by referring to the breed standard of perfection. The standard describes the ideal dog, and those animals that come close to the ideal are generally selected as show stock; those that do not are sold as pets. Keep in mind that pet-quality purebred dogs are in no way less healthy or attractive than show-quality specimens. Sometimes these dogs even prove more hardy. It's just that the pet may have features that would be faults in the show ring. Often these so-called "flaws" are detectable only by experienced breeders or show judges.

One particular Jack Russell Terrier may seem eager to become your pet. Ask to see this one away from his littermates to find out a bit more about his temperament and personality.

Busy families and single adults don't always have the time to take care of a Jack Russell Terrier pup. Consider adopting an adult Jack Russell Terrier instead. Contact your local breed club or veterinarian for rescue organizations in your area.

If you are looking for a pet for the children or a companion for you, an older pup or a grown dog that is not being used for breeding or showing may be available.

The price you pay for your dog is little compared to the love and devotion he will return over the many years he'll be with you. With proper care and affection, your pup should live to a ripe old age; thanks to modern veterinary science and improvements in canine nutrition, dogs today are better maintained and live longer. It is not uncommon to see dogs living well into their teens.

ADULT OR PUP

Whether to buy a grown dog or a young puppy is an important decision. It is an undeniable pleasure to watch your dog grow from a lively pup to a mature, dignified dog. However, if you don't have the time to spend on frequent meals, housetraining, and other training that a puppy needs in order to become a dog you can be proud of, then choose an older, partly trained adolescent or a grown dog. If you want a show dog, remember that no one, not even an expert, can predict with 100-percent accuracy what a puppy will be like when he grows up. Six months of age is the earliest age for the would-be exhibitor to select a prospect and know that his future is in the show ring. If you have a small child, it is best to get a puppy that is not less than four or five months old. Older children will enjoy playing with and helping to take care of a baby pup, but at less than four months of age, a puppy wants to do little else but eat and sleep. He must be protected from teasing and overexcitement. Children must learn how to handle and care for their young pets.

WHAT TO LOOK FOR IN A PUPPY

Make sure that the puppy you are considering comes from healthy, well-bred parents and is friendly and outgoing. If you want a show dog and have no experience in choosing a prospect, study the breed standard and listen carefully to the breeder about the finer points of show conformation. A breeder wants his top-quality show puppies placed in the public eye to reflect on his kennel and to attract future buyers.

The breeder should supply you with registration papers, a pedigree, a health record, and a diet sheet when you purchase your Jack Russell Terrier.

Now that you have made your choice, you are ready to depart with puppy, papers, and instructions. Make sure that you know the youngster's feeding routine and take along some of his food. For the trip home, place him in a comfortable, sturdy carrier. Do not drive home with a puppy on your lap! If you'll be traveling for a few hours, bring along a bottle of water from the breeder and a small water dish.

PEDIGREE AND REGISTRATION

The term "pedigree" is quite different from the term "registration." A pedigree is nothing more than a statement made by the breeder about the dog's lineage, and it will contain the names of several generations from which the new puppy comes. It records your puppy's ancestry and other important data, such as the pup's date of birth, his breed, his sex, his sire and dam, his breeder's name and address, and so on. If your dog has had purebred champions in his background, then the pedigree papers are valuable as evidence of the good breeding behind him; but if the names on the pedigree papers are meaningless, then so are the papers themselves. Just because a dog has a pedigree doesn't necessarily mean he is registered with a kennel club.

Registration papers from the American Kennel Club or the United Kennel Club in the United States or The Kennel Club of Great Britain attest to the fact that the mother and father of your puppy were purebred and that they were registered with a particular club. Normally, every registered dog also has a complete pedigree available. Registration papers, which you receive when you buy a puppy, enable you to register your puppy. Usually, the breeder has registered only the litter, so it is the new owner's responsibility to register and name an individual pup. The papers should be filled out and sent to the appropriate address printed on the application, along with the fee required for the registration. A certificate of registration will then be sent to you.

Pedigree and registration, by the way, have nothing to do with licensing, which is a local regulation. Find out what the local ordinance is in your town or city and how it applies to your dog, then buy a license and keep it on your dog's collar for identification.

The New Family Member

At long last, the day you have all been waiting for will come, and your new puppy will make his grand entrance into your home.

Before you bring your companion to his new residence, however, you must plan carefully for his arrival. Keep in mind that the puppy will need time to adjust to life with a different owner. He may seem a bit apprehensive about the strange surroundings in which he finds himself, having spent the first few weeks of life with his dam and littermates. In a couple of days, with love and patience on your part, the transition will be complete.

The puppy's first impressions are important, and these feelings may very well set the pattern of his future relationship with you. You must be consistent in the way you handle your pet so that he learns what is expected of him.

Some advance preparation is needed before bringing your new Jack Russell Terrier home. Gates need to be placed to restrict the dog's movement in the home.

Your new Jack Russell Terrier needs plenty of time outdoors to exercise. Supervise him at all times to keep him out of trouble.

He must come to trust and respect you as his keeper and master. When you provide him with proper care and attention, you will be rewarded with a loyal companion for many years. If you consider the needs of your puppy before you bring him home and plan accordingly, it will make the change from his former home to his new one easier.

ADVANCE PREPARATION

In preparing for your puppy's arrival, one of the most important things to find out from the seller is how the pup was maintained. What brand of food was offered, and when and how often was the puppy fed? Has the pup been housetrained; if so, what method was employed? At first, continue the routine started by the puppy's original owner; then, gradually, you can make changes that suit you and your lifestyle. If, for example, the puppy has been paper trained, plan to stock up on newspaper or specially made pads. Place these in a selected spot so that your puppy learns to use the designated area as his "bathroom." If you wish to train the puppy to eliminate outdoors, you can gradually move the area closer to the door, and eventually teach the puppy to go outside. Also, keep a supply of the

The New Family Member

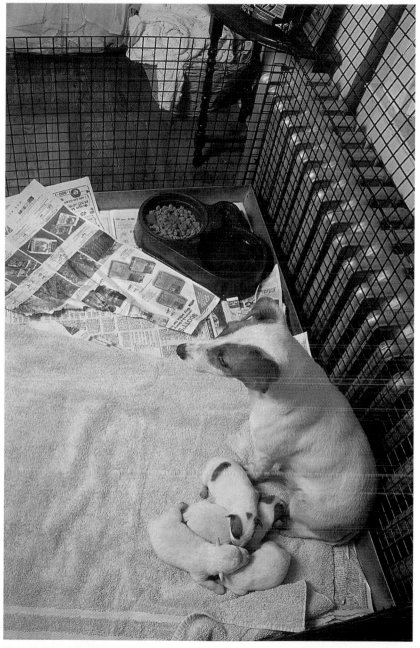

Your Jack Russell Terrier needs a place to call her own. Have a comfortable bed ready for her when she arrives in your home.

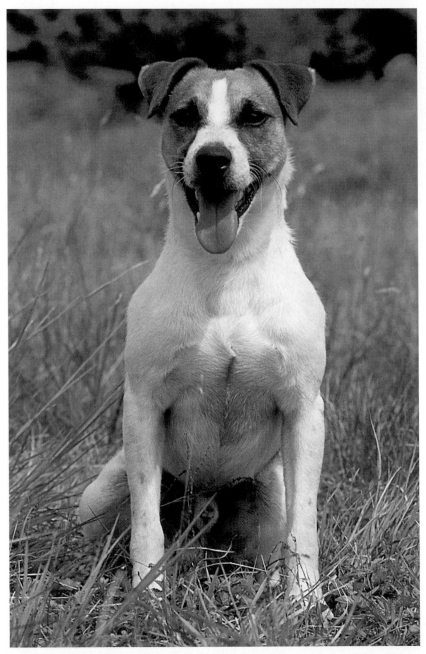

Once he becomes adjusted to living in your home, your Jack Russell Terrier will be a lifelong friend.

dog food he has been eating on hand, because a sudden switch to new food could cause digestive upsets.

Another consideration is sleeping and resting quarters. Be sure to supply a dog bed for your pup and introduce him to his special cozy corner so that he knows where to retire when he feels like taking a snooze. A crate is a great tool to use as your puppy's sleeping quarters, and also aids in the housetraining process. You'll need to buy a collar and leash, safe chew toys, and a few grooming tools as well. A couple of sturdy feeding dishes, one for food and one for water, will be also needed.

FINDING A VETERINARIAN

An important part of your preparations should include finding a local veterinarian who can provide quality health care in the form of routine checkups, inoculations, and prompt medical attention in case of illness or emergency. Find out if the puppy you have selected has been vaccinated against canine diseases and make certain you secure all health certificates at the time of purchase. This information will be valuable to your veterinarian, who will want to know the puppy's complete medical history. Don't wait until your puppy becomes sick before you seek the services of a vet; make an appointment for your

Children should be taught to treat a new Jack Russell Terrier gently and with care for both the dog's and the child's safety.

Adaptable to a variety of lifestyles, this energetic and pleasing dog is an ideal apartment dweller.

pup before or soon after he takes up residence with you so that he starts out with a clean bill of health in his new home.

CHILDREN AND PUPPIES

If you have children at home, be sure to prepare them for the arrival of their new puppy. Children should learn not only to love their charges, but to respect them and treat them with the consideration that one would give all living things. It must be emphasized to youngsters that the puppy has certain needs, just as humans have, and that all family members must take an active role in ensuring that these needs are met. Someone must feed the puppy, walk him a couple of times a day, groom his coat, clean his ears, and clip his nails. Someone must also see to it that the puppy gets sufficient exercise and attention each day.

A child who has a pet to care for learns responsibility; nonetheless, parental guidance is an essential part of this learning experience. You must teach your child how to carefully pick up and handle the pup. A dog should always be supported with both hands, not lifted by the scruff of the neck. One hand should be placed under the chest, between the front legs, and the other hand should support the dog's rear end.

BE A GOOD NEIGHBOR

For the sake of your dog's safety and well-being, don't allow him to wander onto the property of others. Keep him confined to your own yard at all times or on his leash when outside. There are many dangers for an unleashed dog, particularly when he is unsupervised by his master, including cars and trucks, stray animals, and poisonous substances. Also, dogs that are left to roam in a wooded area or field could become infected with any number of parasites. All these things can be avoided if you take precautions to keep your dog in a safe enclosure where he will be protected.

GETTING ACQUAINTED

If possible, plan to bring your new pet home in the morning so that by nightfall he will have had some time to become acquainted with you and his new environment. Avoid introducing the pup to the family around holiday time, because all of the extra excitement will only

Pick up your new Jack Russell Terrier early in the day when you can spend lots of time with him. This will give him plenty of time to explore his new home with you there.

Socialization is very important for your new Jack Russell Terrier. After visiting your veterinarian and beginning the proper inoculations, gradually introduce your dog to other animals and people.

add to the confusion and frighten him. Let the puppy enter your home on a day when the routine is normal. For those people who work during the week, a Saturday morning is an ideal time to bring the puppy to his new home.

Let the puppy explore, under your watchful eye, of course, and let him investigate his new home without stress and fear. Resist the temptation to handle him too much during these first few days. If there are other dogs or animals around the house, make certain that all are properly introduced. If you observe fighting among the animals, you may have to separate all parties until they learn to accept one another. Neglecting your other pets while showering the new puppy with extra attention will only cause animosity and jealousy. Make an effort to pay special attention to the other animals as well.

On that first night, your puppy may be frightened or lonely. It is all right to pay extra attention to him until he becomes used to his surroundings. Some people have had success with putting a doll or a hot

The New Family Member

Lots of love and attention will make your new Jack Russell Terrier adjust to her new home faster.

Give your new Jack Russell Terrier plenty of time to adjust. Patience, praise, and encouragement will help your pup feel welcomed into his new home.

water bottle wrapped in a towel in the puppy's bed as a surrogate mother, while others have placed a ticking alarm clock in the bed to simulate the heartbeat of the pup's dam and littermates. Remember that this furry little fellow is used to the warmth and security of his mother and siblings, so the adjustment to sleeping alone will take time. Select a sleeping location away from drafts and his feeding station. Keep in mind, also, that the bed should be roomy enough for him to stretch out in.

Prior to the pup's arrival, set up his room and partition it with gates or a pen to keep him in a safe enclosure. Wherever you decide to keep him, do it ahead of time so you will have that much less to worry about when your puppy finally moves in with you.

Above all else, be patient with your puppy as he adjusts to life in his new home. If you purchase a pup that is not housetrained, you will have to spend lots of time with him—just as you would with a small child—until he develops proper toilet habits. Even a housetrained puppy may feel nervous in strange new surroundings and have an occasional accident. Praise and encouragement will elicit far better results than punishment or scolding. Remember that your puppy wants nothing more than to please you, and he is anxious to learn the behavior that is required of him.

CHAPTER 7

Feeding Requirements

Perhaps more than any other single aspect of your dog's development, proper feeding requires an educated and responsible dog owner. The importance of nutrition in relation to your dog's bone and muscle growth cannot be overemphasized.

Before you bring your puppy home, ask the seller what food was given and stay with that diet for awhile. If you prefer to switch to some other brand of dog food, begin to add small quantities of the

The number of feedings and the amount fed will vary as your Jack Russell Terrier gets older. Ask your veterinarian or breeder for help in setting up a feeding schedule.

Your Jack Russell Terrier should have manners when it is mealtime. Have your dog assume the sit position until the food is placed on the floor.

new brand to the usual food offering. Make the portions of the new food progressively larger until the pup is weaned from his former diet. This will help to prevent stomach upsets.

What should you feed the puppy and how often? Puppies need to be fed small portions at frequent intervals, because they are growing and their activity level is high. You must ensure that your pup gains weight steadily. As your dog matures, his meals can be made larger and he can be fed once or twice a day, depending on his activity level. As far as the brand of dog food you choose is concerned, a great deal of money and research has resulted in foods that we can serve our dogs with confidence and pride, and most of these commercial foods have been developed along strict guidelines according to the size, weight, and age of your dog. These products are reasonably priced, easy to find, and convenient to store. Just be sure to read the label carefully to determine if the food is right for your dog's age, activity level, and development.

THE PUPPY'S MEALS

After a puppy has been fully weaned from his mother and until approximately three months of age, he needs to be fed four times a day. Offer him small meals that have been softened with water or milk. At six months of age, two meals are sufficient; at one year, a single meal can be given, supplemented with a few dry biscuits in the morning and evening. Always keep a bowl of cool, fresh water on hand to help your dog regulate his body temperature and to aid in digestion.

From one year of age on, you may continue feeding the mature dog a single meal or you may prefer to divide this meal in two, offering half in the morning and the other half at night. Discuss your dog's

Feeding Requirements

Meals should be served at the same time every day. Your Jack Russell Terrier will get used to the schedule that you set.

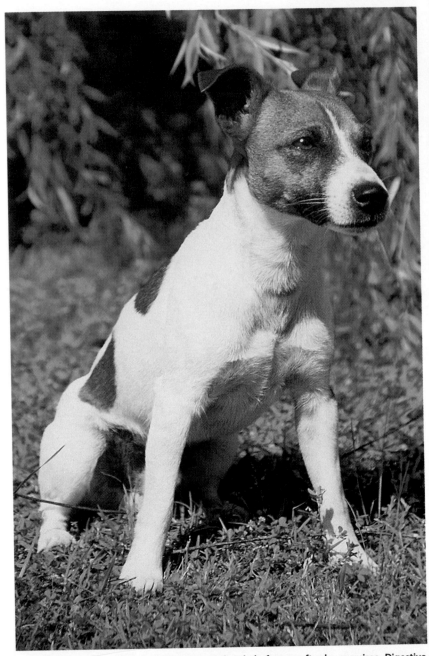

Avoid feeding your Jack Russell Terrier immediately before or after he exercises. Digestive problems may result.

feeding schedule with your veterinarian; he can make suggestions about the right diet for your particular canine friend.

FACTORS AFFECTING NUTRITIONAL NEEDS

Activity Level. A dog that lives in a country environment and is able to exercise for long periods of the day will need more food than the same breed of dog living in an apartment and given little exercise. Likewise, a working country canine would burn up more calories than one that simply lived in the country and received plenty of exercise.

Quality of the Food. Obviously, the quality of food will affect the quantity required by a puppy. If the nutritional content of a food is low, then the puppy will need more of it than a better quality food.

Balance of Nutrients and Vitamins. Feeding a puppy the correct balance of nutrients is not easy, because the average person is not able to measure out ratios of one to another, so it is a case of trying to see that nothing is in excess. However, only tests or your veterinarian can be the source of reliable advice.

Genetic and Biological Variation. Apart from all of the other considerations, it should be remembered that each puppy is an individual. His genetic makeup will influence not only his physical characteristics, but also his metabolic efficiency. This being so, two pups from the same litter can vary quite a bit in the amount of food they need to perform the same function under the same conditions. If you consider the potential combinations of all of these factors, you will see that pups of a given breed could vary quite a bit in the amount of food they will need. Before discussing feeding quantities, it is valuable to know at least a little about the composition of food and its role in the body.

COMPOSITION AND ROLE OF FOOD

The main ingredients of food are protein, fats, and carbohydrates, each of which is needed in relatively large quantities when compared to the need for vitamins and minerals. The other vital ingredient of food is, of course, water. Although all foods obviously contain some of the basic ingredients needed for an animal to survive, they do not all contain the ingredients in the needed ratios or types. For example, there are many forms of protein, just as there are many types of carbohydrates. Both of these compounds are found in meat and in vegetable matter—but not all of those that are needed will be in one particular meat or vegetable. Plants, especially, do not contain

Give your Jack Russell Terrier treats throughout the day, but remember that these treats should be nutritious and are a part of his daily food intake.

certain amino acids that are required for the synthesis of certain proteins needed by dogs.

Likewise, vitamins are found in meat and vegetable matter, but vegetables are a richer source of most. Meat contains very little carbohydrates. Some vitamins can be synthesized by the dog, so they do not need to be supplied via the food. Dogs are omnivores, which means that they digest both meat and vegetable matter.

In order to gain its needed vegetable matter in a form that it can cope with, the carnivore eats all of its prey. This includes the partly digested food within the stomach. In commercially prepared foods, the cellulose is broken down by cooking. During this process, the vitamin content is either greatly reduced or lost altogether. The manufacturer, therefore, adds vitamins once the heat process, has been completed. This is why commercial foods are so useful as part of a feeding regimen, providing they are of good quality and from a company that has prepared the foods very carefully.

Proteins: These are made from amino acids, of which at least ten are essential if a puppy is to maintain healthy growth. Proteins provide the building blocks for the puppy's body. The richest sources are meat, fish, and poultry, together with their by-products. The latter will include milk, cheese, yogurt, fishmeal, and eggs. Vegetable matter that has a high protein content includes soy beans, together with numerous corn and other plant extracts that have been dehydrated. The actual protein content needed in the diet will be determined both by the activity level of the dog and his age. The total protein need will also be influenced by the digestibility factor of the food given.

Fats: These serve numerous roles in the puppy's body. They provide insulation against the cold and help buffer the organs from knocks and general activity shocks. They provide the richest source of energy, and reserves of it, and they are vital in the transport of vitamins and other nutrients, via the blood, to all other organs. Finally, it is the fat content within a diet that gives it palatability, although it is important that it not be excessive. This is because the high energy content of fats (more than twice that of proteins or carbohydrates) will increase the overall energy content of the diet. The puppy will adjust his food intake to that of his energy needs, which are obviously more easily met in a high-energy diet. This will mean that while fats are providing the energy needs of the puppy, the overall diet may not be providing his protein, vitamin, and mineral needs, so signs of protein deficiency will become apparent. Rich sources of fats are those of meat, their by-products (butter, milk), and vegetable oils, such as safflower, olive, corn, or soy bean.

Carbohydrates: These are the principle energy compounds given to puppies and adult dogs. Their inclusion within most commercial brand dog foods is for cost, rather than dietary needs. These compounds are more commonly known as sugars, and they are seen in simple

There are many different types of pet food in the stores today. Try to continue using the brand that was given to your Jack Russell Terrier by the breeder.

or complex compounds of carbon, hydrogen, and oxygen. One of the simple sugars is called glucose, and it is vital to many metabolic processes. When large chains of glucose are created they form compound sugars. One of these is called glycogen, and it is found in the cells of animals. Another, called starch, is the material that is found in the cells of plants.

Vitamins: These are not foods as such but chemical compounds that assist in all aspects of an animal's life. They help in so many ways that to attempt to describe them effectively would require a chapter in itself. Fruits are a rich source of vitamins, as are the livers of most animals. Many vitamins are unstable and easily destroyed by light, heat, moisture, or rancidity. An excess of vitamins, especially A and D, has been proven to be very harmful. Provided a puppy is receiving a balanced diet, it is most unlikely there will be a deficiency, whereas hypervitaminosis (an excess of vitamins) has become quite common due to owners and breeders feeding unneeded supplements. The only time you should feed extra vitamins to your puppy is if your veterinarian advises you to do so.

Minerals: These provide strength to bone and cell tissue, as well as assisting in many metabolic processes. Examples are calcium, phosphorous, copper, iron, magnesium, selenium, potassium, zinc, and

Fresh, clean water is as important to your Jack Russell Terrier's health as nutritious food. Make sure he has plenty of water, especially on hot days.

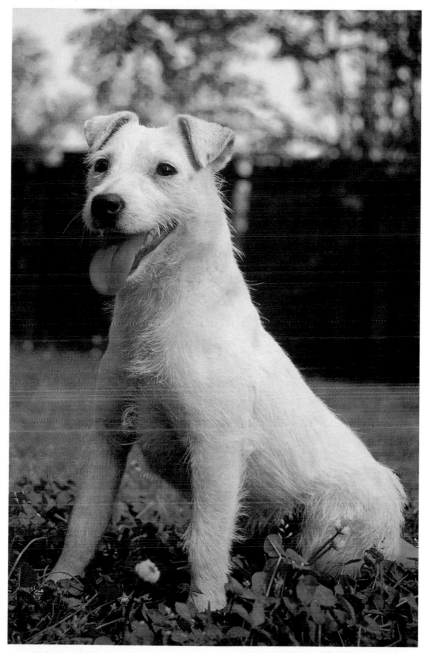

Your Jack Russell Terrier will need to eliminate almost immediately after eating. Take your dog to a potty area when he finishes his meal and praise him when he eliminates.

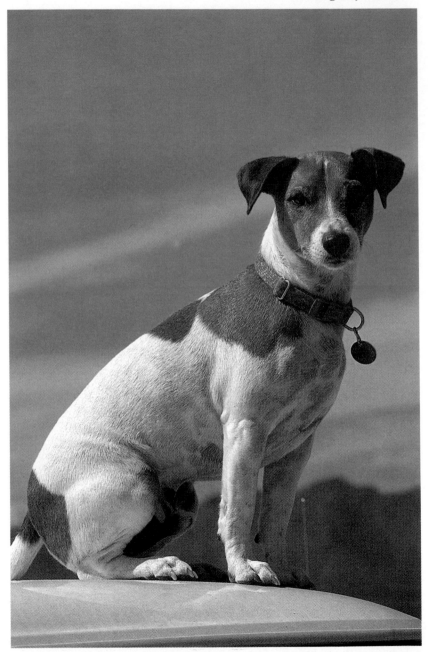

Given the proper diet of a nutritious dog food with a growth formula, your Jack Russell Terrier will grow to be a happy, healthy adult.

sodium. The full dietary need for all minerals has not been fully established. Calcium and phosphorous are known to be important, especially to puppies. They help in forming strong bone. As with vitamins, a mineral deficiency is most unlikely in pups given a good and varied diet. Again, an excess can create problems—this applying particularly to calcium.

Water: This is the most important of all nutrients, as is easily shown by the fact that the adult dog is made up of about 60 percent water, the puppy containing an even higher percentage. Dogs must retain a water balance, which means that the total intake should be balanced by the total output. The intake comes either by direct input (the tap or its equivalent), plus water released when food is oxidized, known as metabolic water (all foods contain the elements hydrogen and oxygen, which recombine in the body to create water). A dog without adequate water will lose condition more rapidly than one depleted of food, a fact common to most animal species.

READING LABELS

There are two agencies that work together in regulating pet food labels. The first agency, the Association of American Feed Control Officials (AAFCO), is a nongovernmental agency made up of state and federal officials from around the United States. They establish pet food regulations that are more specific and cover areas like guaranteed analysis, nutritional adequacy statements, and feeding directions. Each states decides whether or not to enforce AAFCO's regulations—most do; however, some do not.

The second agency, the Food and Drug Administration Center for Veterinary Medicine, establishes and enforces standards for all animal feed. This federal agency oversees aspects of labeling that cover proper identification of product, net quantity statements, and the list of ingredients.

Learning how to read the labels of dog food is important, especially when you consider how many brands are out there. Slight changes in wording can make the difference between a quality dog food and one that may not appear to be what it seems.

PRODUCT NAME

You may think the name of your dog food is just the name—but in this case, it can make a big difference. Specific words used in the name can indicate what is in the food and what is not. For example, a brand name like "Beef Dog Food" must contain at least 95 percent beef, but if it is called "Beef *Formula* for Dogs," it is required to contain a minimum of only 25 percent beef. Other words like dinner, platter, nuggets, or entrée fall under this 25 percent minimum requirement.

Another word to watch for is "with." A dog food called "Dog Food with Beef" only has to contain a minimum of three percent beef. The word "with" was originally supposed to highlight extra ingredients, but recent amendments to AAFCO regulations now allow the word to be used in the product's name. Also, the word "flavored" can be deceiving, because it means that only a sufficient amount of flavoring needs to be added for it to be detectable. Therefore, "Beef Flavored Dog Food" may not include any beef at all and may only be flavored with very small amounts of beef by-products.

INGREDIENT LIST

Each ingredient contained in the dog food will be listed in descending order according to weight, but the quality of the ingredient is not required to be listed. For best results, look for animal-based proteins to be high up on the list, such as beef, beef by-products, chicken, chicken by-products, lamb, lamb meal, fish meal, and egg. However, use caution and read carefully, because some manufacturers will manipulate the weight of products in order to place them higher or lower on the list. For example, they may divide the grains into different categories, like wheat flour and whole ground wheat, in order to lower the weight and make them seem less prominent on the ingredient list.

What exactly are meat by-products and meal, anyway? Actual "meat" is considered to be the clean flesh of a slaughtered mammal and is limited to the part of the striate muscle that is skeletal or found in the tongue, diaphragm, heart, or esophagus. Meat by-products are the nonrendered lean parts other than the meat, which includes, but is not limited to, the lungs, spleen, kidney, bone, blood, stomach, intestines, necks, feet, and undeveloped eggs. Meat and bone meal are the rendered product or mammal tissue, which includes bone, hair hood, horn, hide trimming, manure, and stomach. As you can see, the ingredients in dog food can vary widely, which is why it is so important to be informed about what your puppy is actually eating.

GUARANTEED ANALYSIS

The guaranteed analysis states the minimum amount of crude pro-

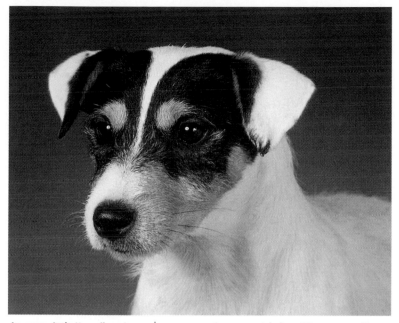

As your Jack Russell matures, he may require a special diet. Discuss any dietary changes with your veterinarian and make them gradually.

tein and crude fat, as well as the maximum amount percentage of moisture (water) and crude fiber. The word "crude" refers to the method of testing the product, not the quality of the nutrient. Sometimes manufactures will list other nutrients like ash or calcium, although they are not required to do so.

NUTRITIONAL ADEQUACY STATEMENT

The nutritional adequacy statement is important when looking for a dog food for puppies, because it states what life stage the product is formulated for, such as growth, reproduction, maintenance, senior, or all life stages. For best results for developing puppies, look for the product that is especially formulated for growth. It should also tell you whether the product is "complete and balanced" or "complementary." Complete and balanced means that it contains all the ingredients that your dog will need on a daily basis and that it can serve by itself as a meal. Complementary means that it is not intended to be used as a meal and must be added to another product to create one.

NET QUANTITY STATEMENT

The net quantity statement shows the weight of the food in the bag or can in pounds and ounces and in metric weight. Be careful, because some companies use 30-pound bags and then only put 25 pounds of food inside.

FEEDING INSTRUCTIONS

The feeding instructions on the dog food label are only suggestions; some dogs will eat more, some will eat less. Also, they are the amounts needed for the entire day, so you can break it up the best way for you and your puppy by dividing how many meals you feed a day by the total amount. If you are not sure how much to feed, start off with the suggested amount and increase or decrease as necessary.

Although dog food labels tell you a lot about a product, there is a lot they don't tell you. For example, some wording used on labels can be misleading. Foods that use the words "gourmet" or "premium" are not required to contain any higher quality ingredients than any other product. Products that claim to be "all-natural" are not required to be so. Some might think that this means that the food is minimally processed or contains no artificial ingredients, but this is not necessarily true. In fact, all dog foods must contain some chemically synthesized ingredients in order to be deemed complete and balanced.

HOMEMADE DIETS

There seems to be a debate about whether a homemade diet is better for your dog than a manufactured dog food. The downside to feeding a homemade diet is that you need to be very careful in order to ensure that you are providing your puppy with all of the nutrients he requires. It also takes a lot of time, effort, and energy to cook a proper diet for your dog on a daily basis.

Those that are in favor of a homemade diet believe that commercial dog foods contain contaminated and unhealthy ingredients and feel that it is worth the effort to give their puppy a homecooked meal.

If you have the time, the money, and the belief that it is important to feed your puppy a homemade diet, make sure you consult your veterinarian who can give you a reputable and nutritionally balanced recipe. Although millions of dogs exist and stay healthy on commercially prepared dog food, the ultimate decision is yours to make.

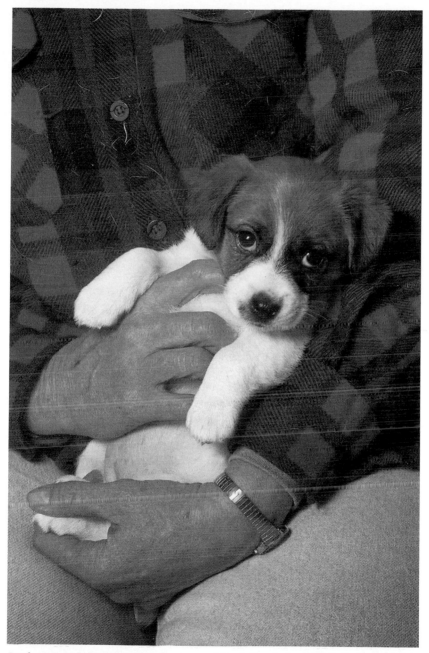

Feed your Jack Russell Terrier the type of food that is formulated for his stage of development and his special needs.

FEEDING GUIDELINES

• Nutritional balance, provided by many commercial dog foods, is vital; avoid feeding a one-sided all-meat diet. Variety in the kinds of meat (beef, lamb, chicken, liver) or cereal grains (wheat, oats, corn) that you offer your dog is of secondary importance compared to the balance or "completeness" of dietary components.

• Always refrigerate opened canned food so that it doesn't spoil. Remember to remove all uneaten portions of canned or moistened food from the feeding dish as soon as the pup has finished his meal. Discard the leftover food immediately and thoroughly wash and dry the feeding dish, as a dirty dish is a breeding ground for harmful germs.

• Always keep a supply of water on hand for your dog. Each day the water dish should be washed with soap and hot water, rinsed well, and dried; a refill of clean, fresh water should be provided daily.

• Food and water should be served at room temperature, neither too hot nor too cold, so that it is more palatable for your puppy.

• Serve your pup's meals in sturdy hard-plastic, stainless steel, or earthenware containers, ones that won't tip over as the dog gulps his food down. Some bowls and dishes are weighted to prevent spillage, while others fit neatly into holders that offer support. Feeding dishes should be large enough to hold each meal.

• As your dog matures, he may need a special diet. Dogs with health problems, such as obesity, pregnant and nursing mothers, and senior dogs all have special dietary needs. Always contact your vet for advice on these requirements.

• Reserve treats for special occasions or to reward good behavior during training sessions. Always make them nutritious.

• Hard foods, such as biscuits and dog meal, should be offered regularly. Chewing on these hard, dry morsels helps the dog keep his teeth clean and his gums conditioned.

• Do not encourage your dog to beg for food from the table while you are eating your meals.

Accommodations

Puppies newly weaned from their mothers and siblings should be kept warm at all times. As they get older, they can be acclimated gradually to cooler temperatures. Although some breeds adapt better to the outdoors than others, all dogs deserve to be allowed to live inside with their families. They also are entitled to a safe outside environment with shelter from the elements. For the time that your

Unless you plan to share your favorite chair with your dog all the time, your Jack Russell Terrier should be trained to stay off of it.

Give your Jack Russell Terrier a place to call his own. His bed should be placed in a warm, dry, draft-free area.

dog will spend indoors, a dog bed in the corner of the family room will suffice, or you may want to invest in a crate for him to "call his home" whenever he needs to be confined for short intervals. You might plan to partition off a special room or part of a room for your pooch, or you may find that a heated garage or finished basement works well as your dog's living quarters. For the time that your dog will spend outside, you may want to buy or build him his own dog house with an attached run or place his house in your fenced-in backyard. All dogs need access to some sort of warm, dry shelter during periods of inclement weather. As you begin thinking about where your canine friend will spend most of his time, you'll want to consider his coat type, his age, his temperament, his need for exercise, and the money, space, and resources you have available to house him.

THE DOG BED

In preparing for your puppy's arrival, it is recommended that a dog bed be waiting for him so that he has a place to sleep and rest. If you have provided him with his own bed or basket, make sure that it is placed in a warm, dry, draft-free spot that is private but at the same

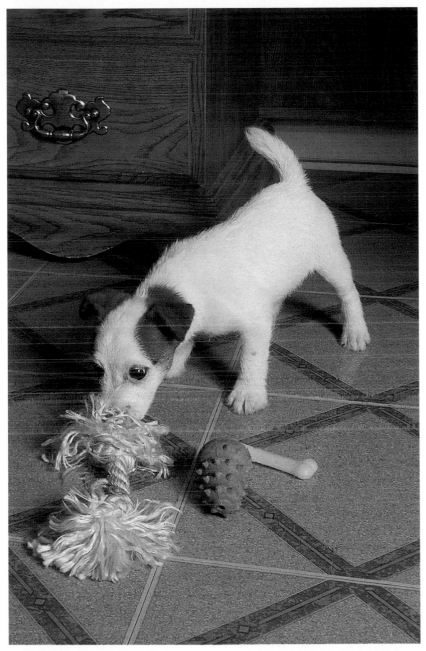

Your Jack Russell Terrier needs toys, such as those made by Nylabone®, to keep him busy. A few toys in his bed may help to keep him from feeling lonely at night.

Your Jack Russell's safety is very important. Keep an eye on him as he explores his new home.

Accommodations

time near the center of family activity. Refrain from placing his bed near his food and water dishes. You may want to give your puppy something to snuggle, such as a laundered towel or blanket or an article of old clothing. Some dogs have been known to chew apart their beds and bedding, but you can easily channel this chewing energy into more constructive behavior by simply supplying him with some safe toys to chew on. Pet shops stock dog beds, among other supplies that you might need for your pup. Select a bed that is roomy, comfortable, and easy to clean, keeping in mind that you

Providing a blanket for your dog will help keep him warm on those cold winter nights.

may have to replace the smaller bed with a larger one as the puppy grows to adulthood. Remember to clean and disinfect the bed and sleeping area regularly.

THE CRATE

Many people cringe at the word crate because they think of it as a cage or a cruel means of confinement. However, this handy piece of equipment can be put to good use for puppies and grown dogs alike. Even though you love your dog, you may not want him to have free reign of the house, particularly when you are not home to supervise him. If used properly, a crate can restrict your dog when it is not convenient to have him underfoot—keeping both the dog and your belongings safe.

A surprising number of dog owners who originally had negative feelings about crating their dogs have had great success using

Changing the pup's bedding if it is soiled or dirty will help to keep him in good health.

crates. The crate can serve as a bed, provided it is furnished with bedding material, or it can be used as an indoor dog house. You can use it to confine your dog for a few hours while you are away from home or at work, or you can bring your crated dog along with you in the car when you travel or go on vacation. Crates also prove handy whenever you have to transport a sick dog to the veterinarian.

Most crates are made of sturdy wire or plastic, and those made by Nylabone® can be conveniently stored or folded so that they can be moved easily. You can allow your puppy or grown dog to become acquainted with his crate by propping the door open and leaving some of his favorite toys inside. He will come to regard it as his own doggie haven in no time. As with a dog bed, place the crate away from drafts in a dry, warm spot and refrain from placing food and water dishes in it, as these only crowd the space and offer opportunity for spillage.

When choosing a crate for your dog, select one in which the dog can stand up and move around comfortably. Never leave the dog confined in his crate for more than a few hours at a time without letting him out to exercise, play, and, if necessary, relieve himself.

Crates can also be a useful tool when housetraining. Because dogs do not like to soil where they eat or sleep, your puppy will wait until

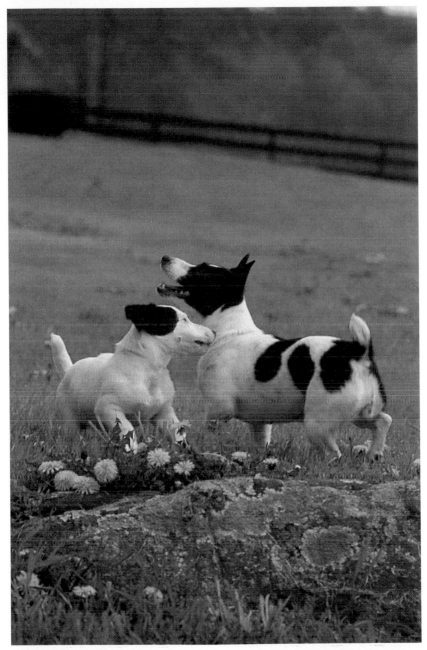

Jack Russell Terriers love to be outdoors. If possible, provide your dog with a dog run or a dog house of his own in your yard.

you take him outside to relieve himself. By confining him in his crate, you are reducing the chances that he will have an accident in the house.

THE DOG HOUSE

These structures, often made of wood, should be sturdy and offer enough room for your dog to stretch out in when he rests or sleeps. Dog houses that are elevated or situated on a platform protect the animal from cold and dampness that may seep through the ground. For the breeds that are hardy and enjoy the outdoors, a dog house in a secure, fenced-in area is an excellent place to keep them if you are not at home during the day.

If you cannot supervise your Jack Russell Terrier, he should be in a fenced-in area that will help keep him safe.

Some fortunate owners whose yards are enclosed by high fences can allow their dogs complete freedom within the boundaries of their property. In these situations, a dog can leave his dog house and get all the exercise he wants. Of course, such a large space requires more effort to keep clean. An alternative to complete backyard freedom is a dog kennel or run that attaches to or surrounds the dog's house. These runs provide ample room for walking, climbing, jumping, and stretching. Another option is to fence off part of the yard and place the dog house in the enclosure.

CLEANLINESS

No matter where your dog lives, either in or out of your home, be sure to keep him in surroundings that are as clean and sanitary as possible. You should clean up after your dog every day. If your dog lives in his own house, the floor should be swept occasionally and the

Accommodations

bedding should be changed regularly. Food and water dishes need to be scrubbed with hot water and detergent and rinsed well to remove all traces of soap. The water dish should be refilled with a constant supply of fresh water. The dog and his environment must be kept free of parasites (especially fleas and mosquitoes, which can carry disease) with products designed to keep these pests under control. Dog crates need frequent scrubbing, too, as do the floors of kennels and runs. Your pet must be kept clean and comfortable at all times; if you exercise strict sanitary control, you will keep disease and parasite infestation to a minimum.

EXERCISE

A well-balanced diet and regular medical attention from a qualified veterinarian are essential in promoting your dog's good health, but so is daily exercise. This keeps him fit and mentally alert. Dogs that have been confined all day while their owners are at work or school need special attention. There should be some time set aside each day for play, as well as walks after each meal so that they can relieve themselves.

Whenever possible, take a stroll to an empty lot, a playground, or a nearby park. Attach a long lead to your dog's collar. This will help him burn calories, keep trim, and relieve tension and stress that may have had a chance to develop while you were away all day.

Young Jack Russell Terrier pups, like all puppies, have no control over their bowels or bladders. Spreading newspaper around the bed will help make the cleanup of accidents easier.

Regular exercise is important to maintaining your Jack Russell Terrier's health.

For people who work during the week, weekend jaunts can be especially beneficial, because you have more time to spend with your canine friend. Games and fun are very important, too, not only for your dog's well-being, but also as a means of creating a strong bond between dogs and owners. You might want to engage your dog in a simple game of fetch with a stick or a rubber ball. Teaching him basic tricks such as rolling over, standing on his hindlegs, or jumping up (all of which can be done inside the home as well) can provide additional exercise. If you plan to challenge your dog with a real workout, remember not to push him too hard without first warming up with a brisk walk. Don't forget to "cool him down" afterward with a rhythmic trot until his heart rate returns to normal. Some dog owners jog with their dogs or take them along on bicycle excursions. Never push your dog too hard; regular extensive training should only be done with adult dogs, never puppies. You should also work up to maximum speed very slowly, working in short time intervals at first, then building up the length of the workouts as your dog improves his condition.

At the very least, however, play with your dog every day to keep him in good shape, physically and mentally. If you can walk him outdoors or better yet run with him in a more vigorous activity, by all means do it. Don't neglect your pet and leave him confined for long periods without giving him attention or time for exercise.

CHAPTER 9

Housetraining and Basic Training

The new addition to your family may already have received some basic housetraining before his arrival in your home. A puppy will want to relieve himself about half a dozen times a day; it is up to you to specify where and when he should do it. Housetraining is your first training concern and should begin the moment you bring the puppy home.

Ideally, a puppy should be taken outdoors to eliminate. The best times to take him outside are first thing in the morning, after each

Potty training will be much easier for your Jack Russell Terrier pup if you continually bring him back to the same spot to eliminate.

meal, after naps, after play times, and before bedtime at night. When he eliminates, he should be praised. He should also be encouraged to use the same area and will probably be attracted to it after frequent use.

You should use the same command when you take your puppy outside so that your pet will associate the act of elimination with a particular word of your choice. Some words to use are "go," "hurry," "potty," or anything else you feel comfortable saying. The shorter the word, the more you can repeat it and imprint it on your dog's memory.

It is important to familiarize yourself with the telltale signs preceding your puppy's elimination process. There is usually a sense of urgency on the dog's part; he may follow a sniffing and circling pattern, which you will soon recognize. Remember that any training takes time. Such a conditioned response can be obtained with intensive practice with any normal, healthy dog over six weeks of age. Patience and persistence will eventually produce results.

Although it is not ideal, some people may prefer to allow their dogs to eliminate in a designated spot inside. In this case, sheets of newspaper or special pads can be used to cover the specific area where your dog should relieve himself. These should be placed some distance away from his sleeping and feeding area, because a puppy will not urinate or defecate where he eats. When the papers or pads are changed, the bottom one should be placed on top of the new ones in order to reinforce the scent. The puppy should be praised during or immediately after he has made use of this particular part of the room. Each positive reinforcement increases the possibility of his using that area again.

When your puppy arrives, it is advisable to limit him to one room, usually the kitchen, as it most likely has a linoleum or easily washable floor surface. If he is given the run of the house, it will be overwhelming and confusing and he might leave his "signature" on your furniture or clothes. There will be time later to familiarize him gradually with his new surroundings.

PATIENCE, PERSISTENCE, AND PRAISE

As with a human baby, you must be patient, tolerant, and understanding of your pet's mistakes, making sure he feels loved and wanted. A young puppy does not have full control of his body functions and does not eliminate on purpose. Never punish the pup for having an accident in the house, especially if you do not catch him

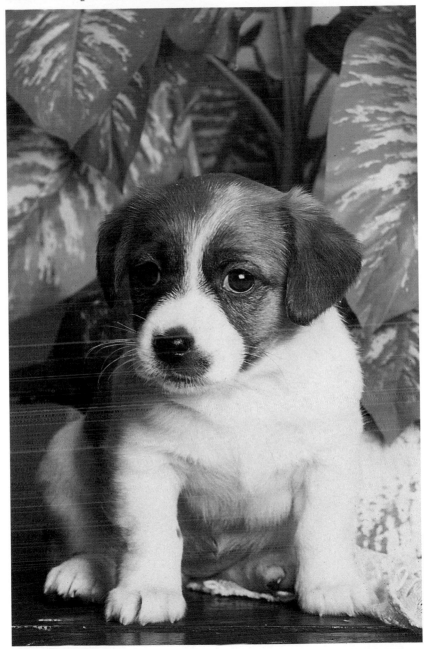

Familiarize yourself with the telltale signs that your pup needs to be taken outside to eliminate.

Praise and reward your Jack Russell Terrier for successfully completing a command. The positive reinforcement and the treat will make him want to continue to please you.

Every dog has the right to be trained. Teach your Jack Russell Terrier exactly which behaviors are tolerated and which ones are not.

in the act. Yelling, hitting, or rubbing his nose in it will teach him only to fear you. If you happen to catch your puppy in the act of eliminating indoors, firmly tell him, "No," and take him outside. If you are diligent about getting him outside often enough, he will soon learn what is expected of him.

Most puppies are eager to please. Praise, encouragement, and reward (particularly the food variety) will produce far better results than any scolding or physical punishment.

Usually, the reason a dog has housetraining or behavior problems is because his owner has allowed them to develop. This is why you must let your dog know what is acceptable and unacceptable behavior from the very beginning. It is also important that you are consistent in your demands; you cannot feed him from the dining room table one day and then punish him when he begs for food from your dinner guests.

TRAINING

You will want the newest member of your family to be a polite dog that is welcomed by everyone. In order to accomplish this, he needs training in the correct forms of behavior. You cannot expect your puppy to become the perfect pet overnight. He needs your help in his socialization process. Training greatly facilitates and enhances the relationship of the dog to his owner and to the rest of society. A successfully trained dog can be taken anywhere and behave well with anyone. Indeed, it is that one crucial word—training—that can transform an aggressive animal into a peaceful, well-behaved pet. Now, how does this "transformation" take place?

Training sessions should always begin and end on a positive note.

WHEN AND HOW TO TRAIN

Like housetraining, training should begin as soon as the puppy enters the house. The formal training sessions should be short but frequent, for example, 10 to 15 minute periods 3 times a day. You are building your relationship with your puppy during these times, so make them as enjoyable as possible. Pick times of the day when your puppy is alert and active. Just before his meals is ideal because he will be more motivated, especially if you reward him with treats.

THE COLLAR AND LEASH

Your puppy should become used to a collar and leash as soon as possible. Have his name and address on an identification tag attached to his collar, as you don't want to lose your pet if he should happen to leave your premises and explore the neighborhood.

Housetraining and Basic Training

Let the puppy wear his collar until he is used to how it feels. After a short time, he will soon become accustomed to it, and you can attach the leash. He might resist your attempts to lead him or simply sit down and refuse to budge. Allow him to wander around with the leash until he begins to get used to the feel of it. Keep in mind that a dog's period of concentration is short, so make training sessions brief and always end on a high note, with play and praise. Most of all, remember that patience is the password to success.

GIVING COMMANDS

When you begin giving your puppy simple commands, make them as short as possible and use the same word with the same meaning at all times. You must be consistent or your puppy will become confused. Do not become impatient with him however many times you have to repeat your command.

COME

One of the most important commands your puppy will learn is to come when called. This is important for his safety. The best way to teach this command is to keep your dog on a long leash. Let him wander and explore for a while, then call him to you. If he comes right away, give him a treat and lots of praise. If he doesn't, do not repeat the command. Just pull him toward you with the leash. When he gets to you, praise him anyway so that he associates coming to you with positive results. A good way to introduce the come command is to call the puppy when his meal is ready. Once this is learned, you can call your pet to you at will, always remembering to praise him for his prompt obedience. This "reward," or positive reinforcement, is a

Your Jack Russell Terrier needs to get used to wearing a collar when going out in public.

crucial part of training. If you use the command, "Come," use it every time. Don't switch to "Come here" or "Come boy," as this will only confuse your dog.

Never punish your dog if he does not come when called. This will teach him to associate coming to you with negative results. Just keep trying, and he will eventually learn that it's in his best interest to come when called.

SIT

The sit command is one of the easiest and most useful commands for your dog to learn, so it is a good idea to begin with it. The only equipment required is a leash, a collar, and a few tasty tidbits. Take your dog out for some exercise before his meal. Have a few nutritious treats that your dog likes with you. After about five minutes, call him to you, and praise him when he arrives. Tell him, "Sit," in a loud, clear voice. As you say the command, take a treat and raise it from in front of his nose to directly over his head. As he follows the treat, he should automatically go into the sit position. Praise him and give him the treat for a job well done. If your dog still won't sit after a few

Your Jack Russell Terrier must be taught that commands must be followed. Never give a command that you are not willing to enforce.

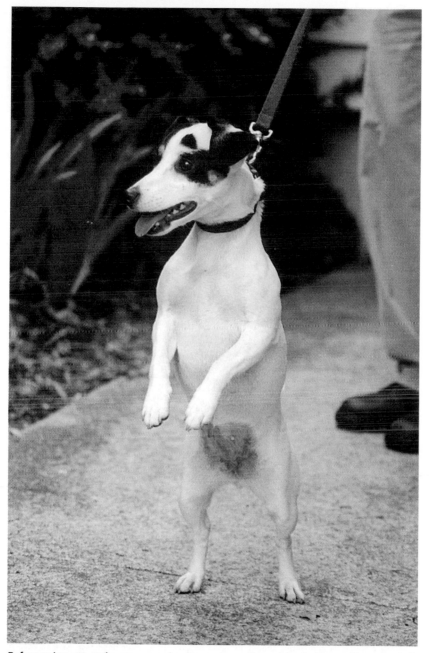

Before going out, make sure your dog has on her collar and leash. Never allow your Jack Russell Terrier to roam or run loose when out in public.

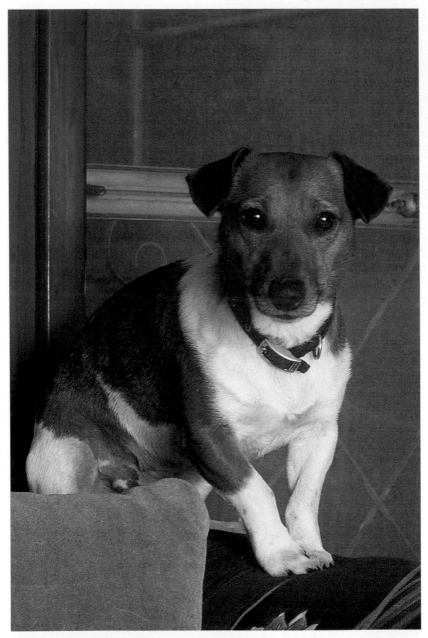

Training commands can begin almost as soon as you bring your new Jack Russell Terrier home. If you allow your dog to get away with misbehavior as a pup, he will not obey as an adult.

tries, tell him, "Sit," and gently press on his rump until he is in a sitting position. As soon as he is in the correct position, praise him and give him the tidbit you have in your hand. Now wait a few minutes to let him rest and repeat the routine. Through repetition, the dog will soon associate the word with the act. Never make the lesson too long. Eventually, your praise will be reward enough for your puppy.

SIT-STAY/STAY

To teach your pet to remain in one place or "stay" on your command, first order him to sit at your side. Lower your left hand with the flat of your palm in front of his nose and your fingers pointing downward. Say, "Sit, stay," and, as you say it, step in front of him. If your dog stays in position, praise him and give him a treat. If he breaks the stay and comes to you, simply place him back in position and try again. This command is especially hard for young puppies, so remember to make the lessons short at first. You can gradually build up the time that your dog stays in position as he matures.

HEEL

When you walk your dog, you should hold the leash firmly in your right hand. The dog should walk on your left, so you have the leash crossing your body. This enables you to have greater control over the dog.

Let your dog lead you for the first few moments so that he fully understands that freedom can be his if he goes about it properly. He already knows that when he wants to go outdoors the leash and collar are necessary, therefore he has respect for the leash.

One of the easiest commands to teach your Jack Russell Terrier is to sit. Most dogs will master it very quickly.

Once the puppy obeys the pull of the leash, half of your training is accomplished. Heeling is a necessity for a well-behaved dog, so teach him to walk beside you, head even with your knee.

To teach your dog this command, start off walking briskly, saying, "Heel," in a firm voice. Pull back with a sharp jerk if he lunges ahead, and if he lags, repeat the command and tug on the leash, not allowing him to drag behind. After the dog has learned to heel at various speeds on leash, you can remove it and practice heeling free, but have it ready to snap on again as soon as he wanders.

DOWN

Teaching the down command ideally begins while your dog is still a pup. During puppyhood, your dog will frequently lie down, as this is one of the dog's most natural positions. Keep close watch over your pup, and each time he begins to lie down, repeat the command, "Down," in a low convincing tone. Eventually, he should associate the motion with the command. Remember to praise him every time he lies down.

Teaching the down command to a mature dog will require more effort. Although the lying position is still natural to a dog, his being

The down command is a difficult one for your dog to learn. The down position in the dog's pack is a sign of being submissive.

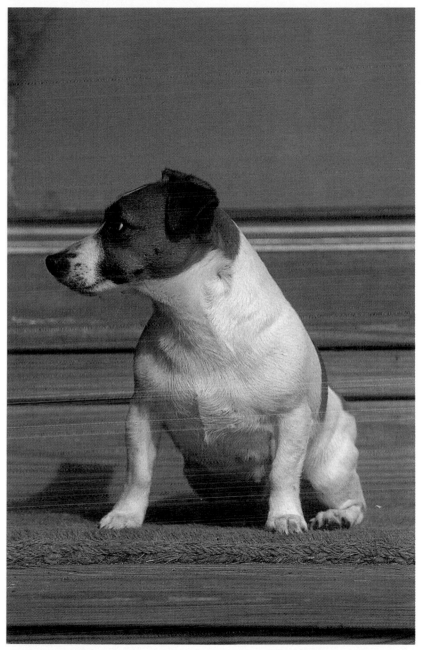

The sit command should be given to your Jack Russell Terrier at the beginning of each training session, because it is the foundation of all the other commands.

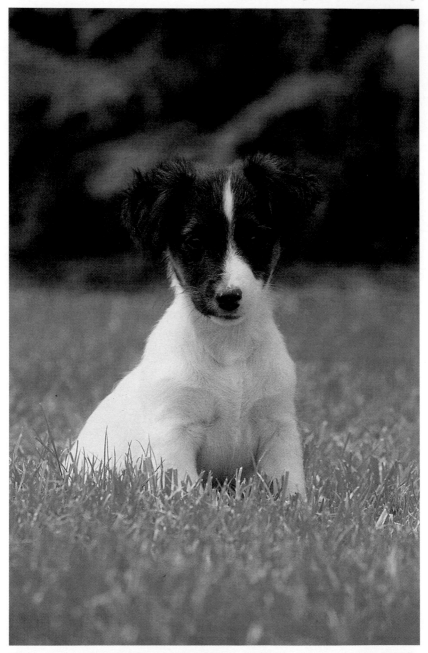

Never scold or yell at your Jack Russell Terrier for not following a command. Simply put him in the last correct position and continue from there.

Training your Jack Russell Terrier for the Canine Good Citizen® Test will ensure that he has good manners and will be welcomed anywhere.

forced into it is not. Have your dog sit and face you. If he is respon sive and congenial, gently take his paws, and slowly pull them toward you; give the down command as he approaches the proper position. Praise him for a job well done. Repeat several times: Moderate reinforcement of this procedure should prove rewardingly successful.

Daily reinforcement of the training method will soon yield the desired results. The keys to remember are: patience, persistence, and praise.

THE CANINE GOOD CITIZEN® TEST

As discussed before, all puppies should have the benefit of basic training. A good way to make sure that your puppy has the good manners he will need is to train for the Canine Good Citizen® Test. The American Kennel Club (AKC) has developed this program to encourage all owners to properly train their dogs. It emphasizes responsible dog ownership and teaching your puppy good manners in the home and in the community. All dogs of any age, purebred or mixed breed, can take the Canine Good Citizen® Test and earn a certificate from the AKC, as well as the right to add the title of CGC® to their names.

Puppies learn the ropes of canine behavior from a parent or older dog. If your adult dog has good habits, they will be passed on to your pup.

The dog must complete ten steps in order to pass. He must prove that he is a dog that any person would like to own, that he is safe with children, that he would be welcomed as a neighbor, and that he makes his owner happy while not making someone else unhappy.

An increasing number of states have now passed Canine Good Citizen® legislation and the CGC® program has been adopted by several other countries.

The American Kennel Club encourages all dog owners to participate in this program. You can find out where a test is being given in your area by contacting your local breed club or the AKC directly.

In order to earn his CGC®, your puppy must pass the following tests:

Test 1: Accepting a Friendly Stranger
This demonstrates that your dog will allow a friendly stranger to approach and speak to you in a natural, everyday situation. You and the evaluator will shake hands and exchange pleasantries. Your dog must show no shyness or sign of resentment and must not break his position and approach the evaluator.

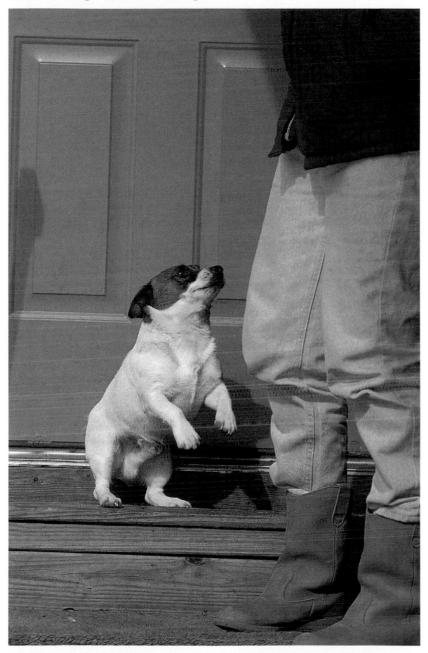

It's never too early to begin training your Jack Russell Terrier puppy. Good training ensures that he will become a well-mannered adult.

You and your dog should not be distracted during a training session. He should be focused on you and your commands the entire time.

Test 2: Sitting Politely for Petting

This test demonstrates your dog's ability to let a friendly stranger touch him while he is out with you. Your dog should sit at your side as the evaluator approaches and pets him on the head or body only. Your dog may stand in place to accept petting and must not show any shyness or resentment.

Test 3: Appearance and Grooming

This practical test demonstrates that your dog will welcome being groomed and examined, and that he will permit a stranger, such as a veterinarian, groomer, or friend of yours, to do so also. It also demonstrates your level of care, concern, and sense of responsibility. The evaluator inspects your dog and combs or brushes him, then lightly examines the ears and each front foot.

Test 4: Walking on a Loose Leash

This test demonstrates that you are in control of the dog. Your dog may be on either side of the handler, whichever you prefer. He must perform a left turn, a right turn, and an about turn, with at least one stop in between and another at the end. Your dog does not have to be perfectly aligned with you and does not need to sit when you stop.

Test 5: Walking Through a Crowd

This test demonstrates that your dog can move about politely in pedestrian traffic and is under control in public places. You and your dog will walk around and pass close to several people (at least three). Your dog may show some interest in the strangers without appearing overexuberant, shy, or resentful. You may talk to the dog and encourage or praise him throughout the test. Your dog should not be straining on the leash.

Test 6: Sit and Down on Command/Staying in Place

This test demonstrates that your dog has had training, will respond to your command to sit and down, and will remain in the place you command him to (sit or down position, whichever you prefer). You may take a reasonable amount of time and use more than one command to make the dog perform the sit and down. When instructed by the evaluator, you must tell your dog to stay and walk forward the length of a 20-foot line. Your dog must remain in place, but may change positions.

Test 7: Coming When Called

This test demonstrates that your dog will come when you call him. You will walk 20 feet away from the dog, then turn to face him and call him to you. You may use encouraging words to get him to come. You may tell your dog to stay or wait, or you may simply walk away, giving no instructions as the evaluator provides mild distractions, such as petting, etc.

Test 8: Reaction to Another Dog

This test demonstrates that your dog can behave politely around other dogs. You and your dog will meet another handler and dog, approach each other from a distance of about ten yards, stop, shake hands and exchange pleasantries, and continue on for about five more yards. The dogs should show no more than a casual interest in one another.

Test 9: Reactions to Distractions

This test demonstrates that your dog is confident when faced with common distracting situations, such as the dropping of a large book or the passing of a jogger in front of the dog. Your dog may express a natural interest and curiosity or appear slightly startled, but should not panic, try to run away, show aggressiveness, or bark.

The Jack Russell Terrier thrives as a companion animal to senior citizens. Her small size and outgoing personality bring a smile to all who meet her.

Test 10: Supervised Separation

This test demonstrates that your dog can be left with a trusted person if necessary and will maintain his training and good manners. Evaluators are encouraged to ask something like, "Would you like me to watch your dog?" and then take hold of the dog's leash. You will then leave your dog's sight for three minutes. Your dog does not have to stay in position, but should not continually bark, whine, or pace unnecessarily, or show anything stronger than mild irritation or nervousness.

EVERYDAY FUN

Not all dog sports have to be organized events. Your puppy will be happy to join you and your family in almost any activity. However, it is important to remember that very young

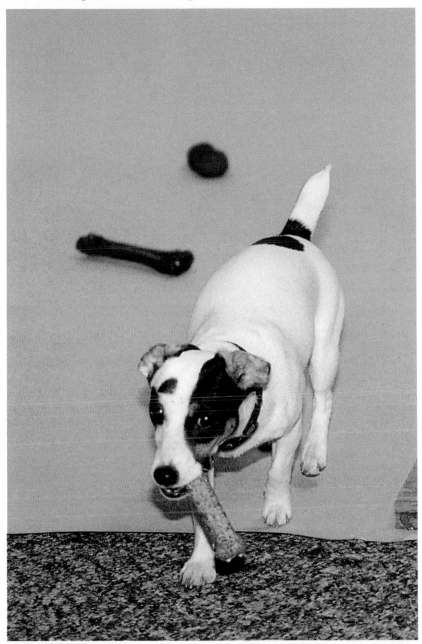

Praise your Jack Russell Terrier for doing things right. Affection in the form of hugs, kind words, or a new chew toy, such as those made by Nylabone®, will reinforce the positive behavior.

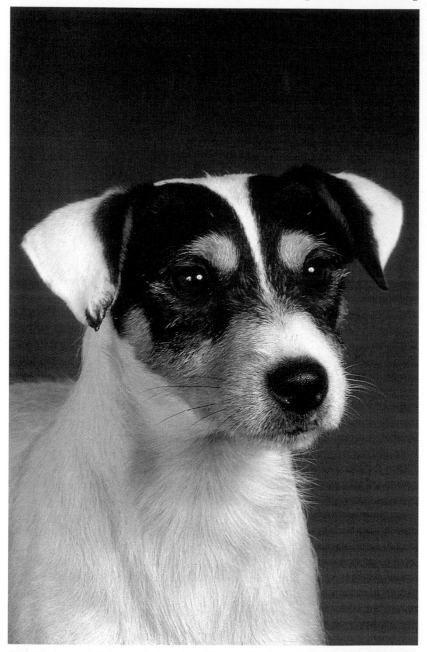

Given the proper training, your Jack Russell Terrier will be a delight to have around.

puppies are still growing; their bones are still soft and they may not be fully developed until they are one year of age or older. Hold off on any serious workouts until your puppy has fully matured physically, or it may cause permanent damage.

Dogs thrive on exercise and will be happy to accompany you jogging, walking, or bicycling. As in any form of exercise, make sure your dog is warmed up first and build up his stamina slowly. If you take the proper precautions, your dog can be in the best physical shape of any conditioned athlete, and you will have a great workout companion.

Show dogs need to learn some special commands and stances. Take your time during training to get it just right.

THERAPY DOGS

There is nothing more rewarding than seeing someone else get as much happiness and delight out of your puppy as you do, and there are some dogs that just seem to love getting a smile out of anyone and everyone. Getting involved with therapy work is a wonderful way to spread the joy of dog ownership to those who may most benefit from it. Statistics show that this aspect of health care is making a real impact and creating some remarkable results with the sick, the elderly, and people with special needs. If your puppy has a particularly even and friendly temperament, therapy work may be perfect for him and especially rewarding for you.

You can have your puppy visit the elderly in nursing homes or patients in hospitals, or you can enroll him in a program that helps educate children about the care and training of dogs. If you contact therapy programs or your local humane society, they can better inform you of programs in your area and the best way to get your puppy started. When your puppy becomes a therapy dog, he is doing more than enriching your life—he is making a valuable contribution to the quality of the life of others.

ASSISTANCE DOGS

Some puppies can be trained to assist people that have physical disabilities. They can help the blind get around independently, help the deaf hear the telephone or the doorbell, and help those confined to wheelchairs accomplish everyday activities, like opening doors or fetching things they need. There are special programs that screen and train these puppies, and some also offer foster programs for people who can take in puppies and train and socialize them until they are ready to be placed with that special person.

SEARCH AND RESCUE DOGS

In almost any city, you will find a search and rescue canine unit. These dedicated handlers and their dogs go to the scenes of disasters and help find survivors and victims. They also help find people who may be lost. They travel great distances and give up much of their time and energy in order to help others—and they do this for the personal sense of satisfaction that they receive, not for money or glory.

It takes a special dog and owner to devote so much of themselves to helping others. Search and rescue dogs come in all different breeds, but all have a few traits in common: athleticism, tracking ability, and perseverance. Getting your dog certified as a search and rescue dog is not easy. You must go through rigorous training exercises under the same conditions that the dog will be facing before you are allowed to actually go to work. The best way to get started is to contact your local law enforcement agency or one of the national associations to see if there are any units in your area. The next time disaster strikes, you and your dog could be helping others—and there is no greater reward of dog ownership.

ORGANIZED DOG SPORTS

Conformation

Everyone thinks that they have a pretty good-looking puppy. If your dog is an AKC-registered purebred and is six months of age or older, you are now ready to jump into the world of dog showing. You may have even purchased your puppy from a breeder with the intention of getting into conformation. In conformation, the main consideration is the dog's overall appearance and structure and how closely he conforms to the standard of the breed.

If you would like to get involved in showing your dog, the first thing you should do is go to dog shows in your area. Spend the day watching not only your breed's judging, but others as well. Judges examine the dogs and place them in accordance to how close each one compares with their mental image of the dog as described in the breed's official standard. These judges are experts in the breed that they are judging. They will examine

Once your Jack Russell Terrier has mastered the basic commands, you may proceed to advanced training and trick training.

each dog with their hands to see if the teeth, muscles, bones, and coat texture match the standard. They also examine each dog in profile for general balance and watch each dog move to see how all these features fit together.

There are three types of conformation shows: the specialty, group, and all-breed. Specialty shows are limited to dogs of a specific breed or grouping of breeds. Group shows are limited to dogs from one of the seven groups; for example, the All-Terrier Show. All-breed shows are open to all of the breeds that are recognized by the AKC. Most dogs in competition at conformation shows are competing for points toward their championships. It takes 15 points, including 2 majors (wins of 3, 4, or 5 points) under at least 3 different judges to become an AKC Champion of Record, which is indicated by a Ch. before the dog's name.

At one show, a dog can earn from one to five points toward a championship title, depending on the number of males or females actually in competition for the breed.

There are six different regular classes in which dogs may be entered. The following classes are offered to male and female dogs separately in each breed entered at the show. Once the dog is a champion, he or she can compete for Best of Breed without having to win in the other classes.

The classes are as follows:

Puppy Class—Open to 6- to 9- or 9- to 12-month-old dogs that are not yet champions.

Twelve to Eighteen Months—Open to 12- to 18-month-old dogs that are not yet champions.

Novice—Open to dogs that have never won a blue ribbon in any of the other classes or that have won less than three ribbons in the novice class.

Bred by Exhibitor—Open to dogs that have been bred by the same person that is exhibiting them.

American Bred—Open to dogs whose parents were mated in America and that were born in America.

Open—Open to any dog of that breed.

After these classes are judged, all the dogs that won first place in the classes compete again to determine which dog is the best of the winning dogs. This is also done separately for male and female dogs. Only the best male (Winners Dog) and the best female (Winners Bitch) receive championship points. A Reserve Winner award is given in each sex to the runner up. The Winners Dog and the Winners Bitch then go onto compete with the champions for the title of Best of Breed. At the end of the Best of Breed competition, three awards are usually given. Best of Breed is given to the dog judged best in his or her breed category. Best of Winners is given to the dog judged as best between the Winners Dog and the Winners Bitch, and Best of Opposite Sex is given to the best dog that is the opposite sex of the Best of Breed winner.

Only the Best of Breed winners advance to compete in the group competition (each breed falls into one of seven group classifications). Four placements are awarded in each group, but only the first place winner advances to the Best in Show competition.

Dog showing can be a very rewarding experience. But be careful—once bitten by the show bug, many people get addicted!

The Jack Russell Terrier's great attitude makes him a natural for conformation and junior showmanship competition.

Junior Showmanship

If your children are interested in training and competing, you may want to get involved in junior showmanship. Junior showmanship evolved as part of the concept that dog shows should be a family sport, as well as entertainment. It was started in the 1930s and has continually grown in participation. It is now an integral part of almost every dog show held in the US and other countries. It is a great way to teach children how to handle, care for, and respect their pets, and also gives them a good start in the sport of dog showing. Participating in junior showmanship is also a great way to foster the relationship between young children and their dogs.

The American Kennel Club rules state that the dog entered in a junior showmanship class must be owned by the junior handler or by one of his relatives or members of his household. Also, every dog entered must be eligible to compete in conformation or obedience, which means the dog must be registered with the AKC. This does not mean that the dog must be of top quality—the rules state that the judges must not judge on the quality of the dog but only on the ability of the junior handler to handle the dog.

The classes are divided into Novice and Open, which are further divided into Novice Junior and Novice Senior, and Open Junior and Open Senior. The Novice Junior class is for boys and girls who are at least 10 but under 14 years of age on the day of the show and who have not won 3 First Place awards in a Novice class at a licensed or member show. The Novice Senior class is for boys and girls who are at least 14 but under 18 years of age and who have not won 3 First Place awards in a Novice class. The Open Junior Class is for boys and girls who are at least 10 but under 14 years of age on the day of the show and who have won 3 First Place awards in a Novice Class. The Open Senior class is for boys and girls who are at least 14 but under 18 years of age on the day of the show and have won 3 First Place awards in a Novice class.

Obedience

You may find that your puppy aced puppy kindergarten and loves to work with you practicing his basic commands. If you have a "workaholic" pup on your hands, obedience may be the right event for you to try.

Obedience trials test your dog's ability to perform a set of exercises. He is then scored on his performance. In each exercise, you must score more than 50 percent of the possible points (ranging from 20 to

40) and get a total score of at least 170 out of a possible 200. Each time your dog gets 170 points, he gets a "leg" toward his title. Three legs and your dog becomes obedience titled. There are three levels at which your dog can earn a title, and each is more difficult than the one before it. You may see levels divided into "A" and "B"; "A" classes are for beginners whose dogs have never received titles, while "B" classes are for more experienced handlers.

The three levels are Novice, Open, and Utility, and the dogs that earn their Utility degrees can go on to compete for their UDX (Utility Dog Excellent) or their OTCh. (Obedience Trial Championship).

Obedience training can also be applied to teaching tricks, like sitting up.

The first level, Novice, will require your dog to demonstrate the skills required of a good canine companion. He will have to heel both on and off leash at different speeds, come when called, stay with a group of other dogs, and stand for a simple physical exam. If your dog passes, he will earn his CD (Companion Dog) title.

The second level, Open, requires your dog to do many of the same exercises as in the Novice class, but off leash and for longer periods of time. There are also jumping and retrieving tasks. If your dog passes, he will earn his CDX (Companion Dog Excellent) title.

The final level, Utility, consists of more difficult exercises, as well as scent discrimination tasks. If your dog passes, he will earn his UD (Utility Dog) title.

Even the youngest puppies can benefit from basic obedience training.

Tracking

All dogs love to use their noses; they use them to communicate with people and other dogs every day. Tracking trials allow dogs to demonstrate their natural abilities to recognize and follow scents. This vigorous outdoor activity is especially great for those canine athletes that have an inherent affinity for tracking, like dogs that are in the hound group, although any dog can participate. Unlike obedience, your dog only has to complete one track in order to earn his title.

There are three titles that a dog can earn in tracking events. The first level is called the TD, or Tracking Dog title. A dog can earn his TD by following a track laid down by a human from 30 minutes to 2 hours before. The rules describe certain turns in a 440- to 500-yard track. The second title, TDX, or Tracking Dog Excellent, is earned by following an older (laid down 3 to 5 hours before) and a longer (800 to 1,000 yards) track with more turns while overcoming both physical and scenting obstacles. A dog that has earned his VST, or Variable Surface Tracking title, has demonstrated his ability to track through urban and wilderness settings by successfully following a three- to five-hour-old track that may take him down a street, through buildings, or through other areas devoid of vegetation.

A good way to get your dog started in tracking is to teach him to play hide and seek in the house. Teach him the name of a certain toy that he likes, such as a ball. First, hide the ball, but let him see where you put it. Then tell him to "find" it. After he gets the hang of what he's supposed to do, have someone keep him in another room while you hide the object. You can make the game increasingly difficult by teaching him to find different objects. If he enjoys playing hide and seek, you probably have a natural tracking dog on your hands.

Agility
One of the most popular, fastest growing, and fun events in the US is agility. It was developed and introduced by John Varley and Peter

Training sessions should be enjoyable for both dog and owner. Make his experiences fun and he will be more likely to obey your commands.

Meanwell in 1978 in England as an entertaining diversion between judgings at a dog show, but was officially recognized as a sport by the AKC in the early '80s. Agility is an exciting sport in which you guide your dog off-lead using verbal commands and hand signals over a series of obstacles on a timed course.

The titles that your dog can earn at an agility trial are Novice Agility Dog (NAD), Open Agility Dog (OAD), Agility Dog Excellent (ADX), and Master Agility Excellent (MAX). In order to acquire an agility title, your dog must earn a qualifying score in his respective class on three separate occasions under two different judges. The MAX title is awarded after the dog earns ten qualifying scores in the Agility Excellent Class.

The only problem with training your puppy to compete in agility is finding the equipment and space for training. Many agility clubs can provide information on getting your puppy started toward an agility title. And even if he doesn't compete, just training for agility can be lots of fun for both you and your dog.

Flyball

Is your puppy an athletic, active dog with a special affinity for tennis balls? If so, flyball may be the right sport for him. Flyball is a relay race between two teams of four dogs and four handlers. Each one of the dogs takes a turn at running over a course that includes four jumps with a flyball box at the end of the course. The dog presses a

If your Jack Russell Terrier has strong retrieving and tracking skills, he might excel at Frisbee™ competitions.

pedal on the front of a flyball box, which releases a throwing arm that sends a tennis ball up in the air. The dog catches the ball and runs back over the course to the starting line. Then another dog takes his turn. The first team to have four dogs successfully complete the course is declared the winner. It is an exciting sport, and you may find that it allows your puppy to use the right combination of his abilities and turns them into a pastime that's fun for all involved.

Frisbee™

Some dogs just love to play with their Frisbees™; they sleep with them, eat with them, and live to play the next game of fetch. People have taken this natural love and developed a sport that allows dogs to display their amazing athletic aptitude. It all started in the mid-1970s when Alex Stein ran out on the field in the middle of a Dodgers baseball game and performed with his Frisbee™ dog, Ashley Whippet. A nationwide audience got to enjoy the high-flying demonstration on television, and the sport of canine Frisbee™ was born. Both mixed breed and purebred dogs can compete, but dogs that excel in Frisbee™ are the medium-sized, lean, agile dogs that are able to take flying leaps and use their owners as launching pads. Other characteristics that make a good Frisbee™ dog are strong retrieving and tracking instincts, an even temperament, and sound hips.

Frisbee™ competitions are held all over the country. They are divided into beginner and intermediate levels, each consisting of two different events. The first event is called the mini-distance, which is played on a 20-yard field. Competitors are given 60 seconds to make as many throws and catches as possible. The second event is the free-flight event, which consists of a choreographed series of acrobatic moves to music. Judges award points on a 1 to 10 scale in each of the following categories: degree of difficulty; execution; leaping agility; and showmanship. Bonus points can be given to competitors with spectacular or innovative free-flight moves.

Friskies and Alpo sponsor over 100 community contests throughout the country each year. There are also seven regional qualifying tournaments culminating in the invitational World Finals in the mall in Washington, DC.

Health Care

INOCULATIONS

Periodic checkups by your veterinarian throughout your puppy's life are good health insurance. Your dog's breeder or previous owner should tell you what inoculations your dog has had and when the next visit to the vet is necessary. You must make certain that your

Plenty of exercise every day will keep your Jack Russell Terrier fit and healthy.

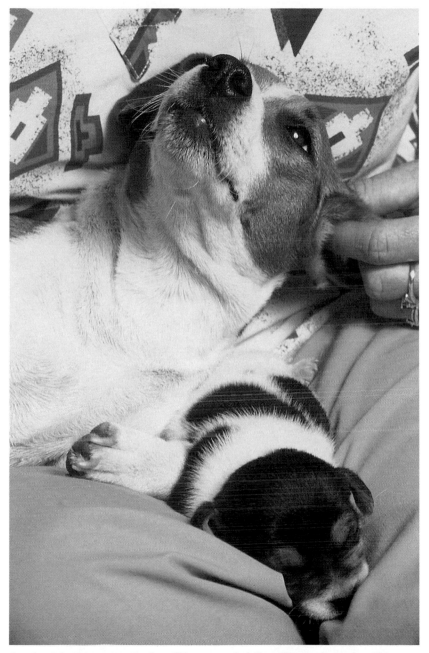

Regular visits to your veterinarian will keep your Jack Russell Terrier in good condition.

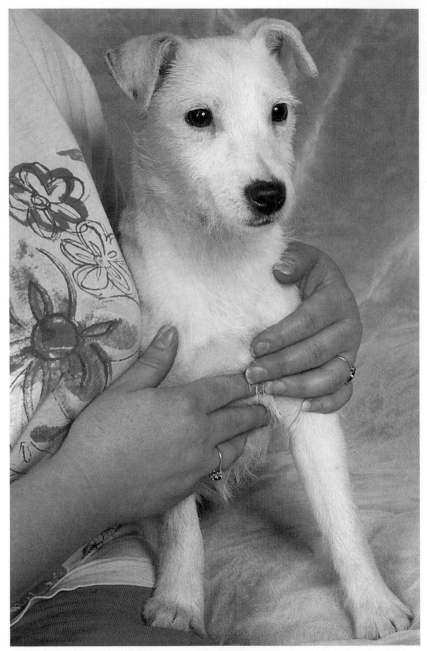

Regular grooming sessions will keep your Jack Russell Terrier looking and feeling his best. Check for any skin problems or parasites while brushing his coat.

Make sure that your Jack Russell has plenty of water if you leave him outside, especially on very warm days.

puppy has been vaccinated against the following infectious canine diseases: distemper, canine hepatitis, leptospirosis, rabies, parvovirus, and parainfluenza. Annual boosters provide your dog with protection against such serious diseases. Puppies should also be checked for worms at an early age.

DISTEMPER

Young dogs are most susceptible to distemper, although it may affect dogs of all ages. Some signs of the disease are loss of appetite, depression, chills, and fever, as well as a watery discharge from the eyes and nose. Unless treated promptly, the disease goes into advanced stages and can cause infection in the lungs, intestines, and nervous system. Early inoculations in puppyhood should be followed by an annual booster to help protect against this disease.

CANINE HEPATITIS

The signs of hepatitis are drowsiness, loss of appetite, high temperature, and excessive thirst. These signs may be accompanied by swelling of the head, neck, and abdomen. Vomiting may also occur.

This disease strikes quickly, and death may occur in only a few hours. An annual booster shot is needed after the initial series of puppy shots.

LEPTOSPIROSIS

Leptospirosis is caused by either of two serovars, canicola or copehageni, and is usually caught because the dog has licked substances contaminated by the urine or feces of infected animals. The signs of leptospirosis are weakness, vomiting, and a yellowish discoloration of the jaws, teeth, and tongue, caused by an inflammation of the kidneys. The frequency of the inoculation is determined by the risk factor involved.

RABIES

Rabies, a disease of the dog's central nervous system, is spread by infectious saliva, which is transmitted by the bite of an infected animal. The dog may show signs of melancholy or depression, then irritation, and finally paralysis. The first period can last from a few hours to several days. After the signs of rabies appear, no cure is possible. The local health department must be notified about any rabid dog, for he is a danger to all who come near him. As with other shots each year, an annual rabies inoculation is very important. In many areas, the administration of rabies vaccines for dogs is required by law.

PARVOVIRUS

Parvovirus is a contagious disease that has spread in almost epidemic proportions throughout certain sections of the United States. It has also appeared in Australia, Canada, and Europe. Canine parvovirus attacks the intestinal tract, white blood cells, and heart muscle. It is believed to spread through dog-to-dog contact, and the specific course of infection seems to come from the fecal matter of infected dogs. Overcoming parvovirus is difficult, for it is capable of existing in the environment for many months under varying conditions and temperatures, and it can be transmitted from place to place on the hair and feet of infected dogs, as well as on the clothes and shoes of people.

A series of shots administered by a veterinarian is the best preventive measure for canine parvovirus.

LYME DISEASE

Known as a bacterial infection, Lyme disease is transmitted by ticks infected with a spirochete known as *Borrelia burgdorferi*. The

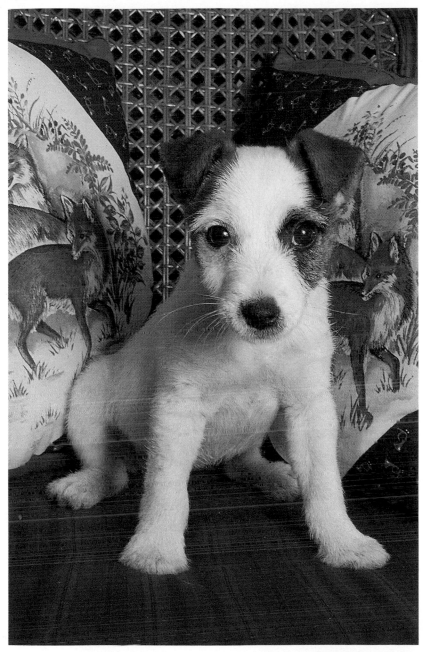

Lots of love and proper care will keep your Jack Russell Terrier with you for many happy years.

disease is most often acquired by the parasitic bite of an infected deer tick, *Ixodes dammini*. While the range of symptoms is broad, common warning signs include a rash beginning at the bite and soon extending in a bullseye-targetlike fashion, chills, fever, lack of balance, lethargy, stiffness, swelling, pain (especially in the joints), heart problems, weak limbs, facial paralysis, and lack of tactile sensation.

Concerned dog owners, especially those living in certain areas of the United States, should contact a veterinarian to discuss Lyme disease. A vaccination has been developed and is routinely administered to puppies twice before the 16th week, then repeated annually.

PARAINFLUENZA

Parainfluenza, or infectious canine tracheobronchitis, is commonly known as "kennel cough." It is highly contagious, affects the upper respiratory system, and is spread through direct or indirect contact with already diseased dogs. It will readily infect dogs of all ages that have not been vaccinated or that were previously infected. While this condition is definitely one of the more serious diseases in dogs, it is self-limiting, usually lasting only two to four weeks. The symptoms are

Jack Russell Terriers love to play outside. When your dog is done playing, examine his coat for ticks and other parasites that may irritate the skin and transmit diseases.

Your Jack Russell Terrier can pick up diseases from other dogs, so be careful when out for your daily walk.

high fever and intense, harsh coughing. As long as your pet sees your veterinarian immediately, the chances for his complete recovery are excellent.

Because this disease is easily spread from dog to dog, it is recommended that your dog get a parainfluenza vaccine before being kenneled or in situations where he would be surrounded by other dogs.

EXTERNAL PARASITES

A parasite is an organism that lives in or on an organism of another species, known as the host, without contributing to the well-being of the host.

Ticks can cause serious problems for dogs. They are usually found in wooded areas or in fields and attach themselves to animals passing by. They have eight legs and a heavy shield or shell-like covering on their upper surface. The only way to prevent your dog from acquiring ticks is to keep him away from tick-infested areas.

The flea is the single most common cause of skin and coat problems in dogs. There are 11,000 kinds of fleas that can transmit specific disorders like tapeworm and heartworm or transport smaller parasites onto your dog. The common tapeworm, for example, requires the flea as an intermediate host for completion of its life cycle.

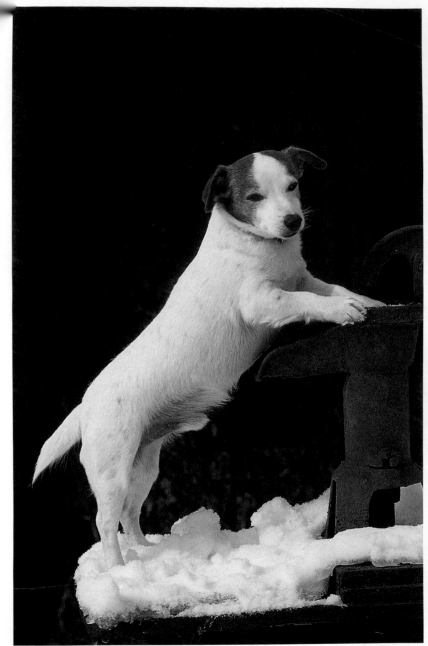

A general knowledge of first aid will help you to ensure the safety of your dog in a home emergency.

A female flea can lay hundreds of eggs and these will become adults in less than three weeks. Depending on temperature and amount of moisture, large numbers of fleas can attack dogs.

Fleas can lurk in crevices and cracks, carpets, and bedding for months, so frequent cleaning of your dog's environment is absolutely essential. If he is infected by other dogs, have him bathed and "dipped," which means that he will be put into water containing a chemical that kills fleas. Your veterinarian will advise which dip to use. Fleas are tenacious and remarkably agile creatures; they have existed since prehistoric times and have been found in arctic as well as tropical climates. Treating your pet for parasites without simultaneously treating the environment is ineffective.

INTERNAL PARASITES

Four common internal parasites that may infect a dog are roundworms, hookworms, whipworms, and tapeworms. The first three can be diagnosed by laboratory examination of the dog's stool, and tapeworms can be seen in the stool or attached to the hair around the anus. When a veterinarian determines what type of worm or worms are present, he then can advise the best treatment.

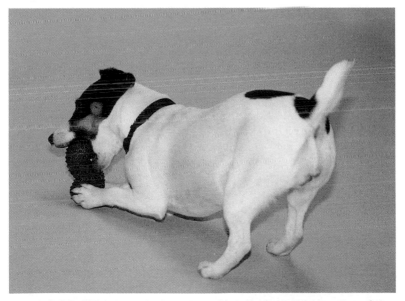

Your Jack Russell Terrier needs chew toys to keep her busy. Have a variety of toys available so your dog does not become bored.

Roundworms, the dog's most common intestinal parasite, have a life cycle that permits complete eradication by worming twice, ten days apart. The first worming will remove all adults and the second will destroy all subsequently hatched eggs before they, in turn, can produce more parasites.

A dog in good physical condition is less susceptible to worm infestation. Proper sanitation and a nutritious diet help in preventing worms. One of the best preventive measures is to have clean, dry bedding for the dog, because this diminishes the possibility of reinfection due to flea or tick bites.

Heartworm infestation in dogs is transmitted by mosquitoes. Dogs with this disease tire easily, have difficulty breathing, and lose weight despite a hearty appetite. Administration of preventive medicine throughout the spring, summer, and fall months is advised. A veterinarian must first take a blood sample from the dog to test for the presence of the disease, and if the dog is heartworm-free, pills or liquid medicine can be prescribed to protect against any infestation.

FIRST AID

Just as you would keep a first aid kit handy for minor injuries sustained by members of your family at home, so you should keep a similar kit prepared for your pet.

In case your dog receives an injury, your kit should contain medicated powder, gauze bandages, and adhesive tape. If the cut is deep and bleeding profusely, the bandage should be applied very tightly to help form a clot. A tight bandage should not be kept in place longer than necessary, so take your pet to the veterinarian immediately.

Walking or running on a cut pad prevents the cut from healing. Proper suturing of the cut and regular changing of the bandages should have your pet's wound healed in a week to ten days. A minor cut should be covered with a light bandage so that as much air as possible reaches the wound.

You should also keep some hydrogen peroxide available, as it is useful in cleaning wounds. Cotton applicator swabs are useful for applying ointment or removing debris from the eyes. A pair of tweezers should also be kept handy for removing foreign bodies from the dog's neck, head, or body.

It is also important to take your dog's temperature at the first sign of illness. To do this, you will need a rectal thermometer, which should be lubricated with petroleum jelly. The normal temperature for a dog is between 101° and 102.5°F.

Danger can be present in your home or yard. If your Jack Russell Terrier should have an accident, contact your veterinarian immediately.

DANGER IN THE HOME

There are numerous household products that can prove fatal if ingested by your pet. These include rat poison, antifreeze, boric acid, hand soap, detergents, insecticides, mothballs, household cleansers, bleaches, de-icers, polishes and disinfectants, paint and varnish removers, acetone, turpentine, and even health and beauty aids if ingested in large enough quantities. A word to the wise should be sufficient: What you would keep locked away from your two-year-old child should also be kept hidden from your pet.

There are other dangers lurking within the home among the household plants, some of which are poisonous, even if swallowed in small quantities. There are hundreds of poisonous plants around us, including ivy leaves, cyclamen, lily of the valley, rhododendrons, tulip bulbs, azalea, wisteria, poinsettia leaves, mistletoe, daffodils, delphiniums, foxglove leaves, and jimson weed. Rhubarb leaves, for example, either raw or cooked, can cause death or violent convulsions. Peach, elderberry, and cherry trees can cause cyanide poisoning if their barks are consumed.

Everything is exciting and new to a Jack Russell Terrier. Let your dog have many happy and safe experiences.

There are also many insects that can be dangerous to dogs, such as spiders, bees, wasps, and some flies. A few toads and frogs exude a fluid that can make a dog foam at the mouth—and even kill him—if he bites too hard!

There also have been cases of dogs suffering nicotine poisoning by consuming the contents of full ashtrays. Do not leave nails, staples, pins, or other sharp objects lying around. Likewise, don't let your puppy play with plastic bags, which could suffocate him. Unplug, remove, or cover any electrical cords or wires near your dog. Chewing live wires could lead to severe mouth burns or death. Remember that an ounce of prevention is worth a pound of cure: Keep all potentially dangerous objects out of your pet's reach.

VEHICLE TRAVEL SAFETY

A dog should never be left alone in a car. It takes only a few minutes for the heat to become unbearable in the summer and to drop to freezing in the winter.

When you cannot supervise your Jack Russell Terrier, make sure he is secure. Accidents can happen when your dog is allowed to run freely.

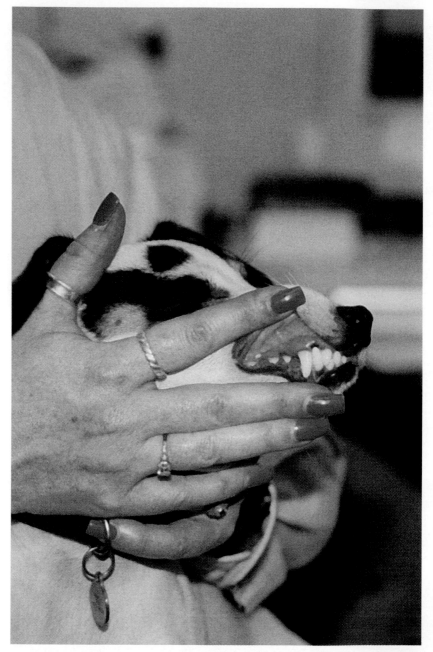

Your Jack Russell Terrier's teeth should be examined periodically. If you notice excessive tartar and plaque buildup, visit your veterinarian to have the dog's teeth professionally cleaned.

To maintain his good health, your Jack Russell Terrier should be immunized against contagious diseases.

A dog traveling in a car or truck should be well behaved. An undisciplined dog can be deadly in a moving vehicle. Allowing him to stick his head out of the window is unwise. The dog may jump out or he may get something in his eye. Some manufacturers sell seat belts and car seats designed for dogs.

Traveling with your dog in the back of your pick up truck is an unacceptable notion and dangerous to all involved.

PROTECT YOURSELF FIRST

In almost all first aid situations, the dog is in pain. He may indeed be in shock and not appear to be suffering until you move him. Then he may bite your hand or resist being helped at all. If you want to help your dog, help yourself first by tying his mouth closed. To do this, use a piece of strong cloth about four inches wide and three feet long, depending on the size of the dog. Make a loop in the middle of the strip and slip it over his nose, with the knot under his chin and over the bony part of his nose. Pull it tight and bring the ends back around his head behind the ears and tie it tightly, ending with a bow

Your Jack Russell Terrier will occasionally require medication. Follow the instructions given by your veterinarian for administering the proper dosage. Sometimes hiding the medication in a treat or meal is the best way to get your dog to take his medicine.

knot for quick, easy release. Now you can handle the dog safely; however, do not leave the emergency muzzle on any longer than necessary.

ADMINISTERING MEDICINE

When you are giving liquid medicine to your dog, pull the lips away from the side of the mouth, form a lip pocket, and let the liquid trickle past the tongue. Hold his muzzle until he swallows. Never pour liquid medicine while the victim's tongue is drawn out, as inhalation pneumonia could result.

Pills are best administered by hiding them in a food treat, such as a piece of cheese or hot dog. The dog will usually gulp down the treat along with the medicine.

ACCIDENTS

It is often difficult to assess a dog's injuries after a road accident. He may appear normal, but there might be internal hemorrhaging. A vital organ could be damaged or ribs broken. Keep the dog as quiet and warm as possible; cover him with blankets or your coat to let his own

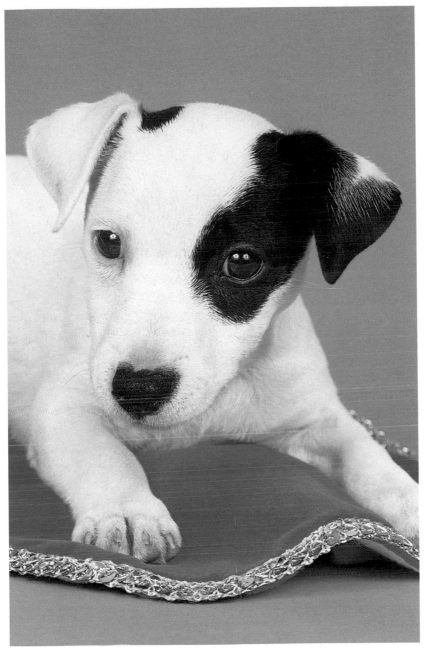

Jack Russell Terriers are very intelligent dogs that are physically fit and easy to train. You owe it to your dog to take proper care of him.

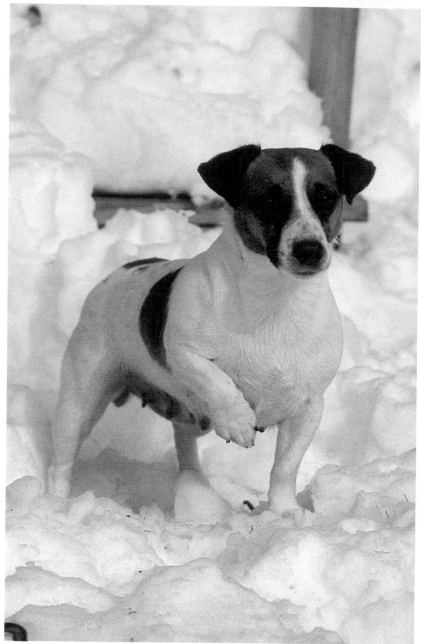

Your Jack Russell Terrier needs you more than ever as she gets older. The mature dog may need extra care and attention to stay healthy.

bodyheat build up. Signs of shock are a rapid and weak pulse, glassy-eyed appearance, subnormal temperature, and slow capillary refill time. To determine if your dog is suffering from slow capillary refill, press firmly against the dog's gums until they turn white. Release and count the number of seconds until the gums return to their normal color. If it is more than two to three seconds, the dog may be going into shock. Failure to return to the reddish pink color indicates that the dog may be in serious trouble and needs immediate assistance.

If artificial respiration is required, first open the dog's mouth and check for obstructions; extend his tongue and examine the pharynx. Clear his mouth and hold slightly open. Mouth-to-mouth resuscitation involves holding the dog's tongue to the bottom of his mouth with one hand and sealing his nostrils with the other while you blow into his mouth. Watch for his chest to rise with each inflation. Repeat every 5–6 seconds, the equivalent of 10–12 breaths a minute.

You need to get your dog to your veterinarian or emergency clinic immediately. Make a stretcher to carry the dog on. To carry a puppy, wrap him in a blanket that has been folded into several thicknesses. If he is in shock, it is better to pick him up by holding one hand under his chest and the other under the hindquarters. This will keep him stretched out.

It is always better to roll an injured dog than to try to lift him. First, apply a muzzle. Then, send someone for a blanket and roll him gently onto it. Two people, one on each side, can make a stretcher out of the blanket and move the dog easily. Try to move him as little as possible.

If no blanket is available and the injured dog must be moved, try to keep him as flat as possible. Get medical assistance for him immediately.

It should be mentioned that car accidents can be avoided if your dog is confined at all times, either indoors or in a fenced-in yard or some other protective enclosure. Never allow your dog to roam free; even a well-trained dog may dart into the street—and the result could be tragic.

Always leash your dog so that he will be protected from moving vehicles.

ILLNESS

It is important to watch for any telltale signs of illness so that you can spare your pet any unnecessary suffering. Your dog's eyes, for example, should normally be bright and alert, so watch for signs of illness or irritation. If your dog has matter in the corners of his eyes, bathe them with a mild eye wash; obtain ointment or eye drops from your veterinarian to treat a chronic condition.

If your dog scratches at his ears or shakes his head, he may have an ear infection. Regular cleaning of the outer ear can help keep your dog's ears clean and free of waxy buildup. If your dog's ears have dirt or dried blood in them, it is indicative of ear mites or infection and should be treated immediately by a vet. Sore ears due to insect bites should be washed with mild soap and water, then covered with a soothing ointment and wrapped in gauze if necessary.

CANINE SENIOR CITIZENS

The processes of aging and gradual degenerative changes start far earlier in a dog than often observed, usually by about seven years of age. Your pet may become less active and may have a poorer appetite with increased thirst. His skin and coat might become dull and dry and his hair may become thin. There is a tendency toward obesity in old age in some breeds, which should be avoided by maintaining a regular exercise program. Remember, also, that your pet will be less able to cope with extreme heat, cold, fatigue, and change in routine.

There is the possibility that your dog may suffer from hearing or eyesight impairment. Other ailments such as rheumatism, arthritis, kidney infections, heart disease, male prostatism, and hip dysplasia may occur. Of course, all of these require a veterinarian's examination

Check with your veterinarian for special care instructions for your Jack Russell Terrier as he gets older.

and recommendation of suitable treatment. Care of the teeth is also important in the aging dog. Indeed, the mouth can be a barometer of nutritional health. Degenerating gums, heavy tartar on the teeth, loose teeth, and sore lips are common. The worst of all diseases in old age, however, is neglect. Good care in early life will have its effect on your dog's later years; the nutrition and general health care of his first few years can determine his lifespan and the quality of his life.

DEATH OF A FRIEND

The companionship of pets, not only to children and adults, but particularly to the aged and lonely, cannot be overestimated. Therefore, a dog's grateful owner should do all he can to enhance and prolong the life of his cherished companion. Regular doses of TLC (Tender Loving Care) are the best "medicine" your dog can receive throughout his life.

What can you do, however, for a pet who is so sick or severely injured that he will never recover his normal health? Although one is often extremely reluctant to consider the suggestion, sometimes the kindest and most humane solution is to have your veterinarian put him out of his misery by inducing his death peacefully and painlessly. This process is called euthanasia, a word of Greek derivation meaning "easy or good death." It is usually carried out by having your veterinarian inject a death-inducing drug or an overdose of anesthetic.

Such a decision will probably be a difficult one for you to make, but you need not, in fact, should not, make it alone. Your veterinarian should be your chief adviser, and family and friends can assist in the decision-making process. Your children should not be excluded from this painful time; it would be inadvisable to attempt to "shield" or "protect" them from such events, which are an inevitable part of life. They would suffer even more if, later, they did not understand how or why their beloved pet had died.

By remembering the wonderful times with your pet, by talking about him to family and friends, by remembering him as healthy and full of life, you will eventually cope with your grief. It is perfectly natural to grieve for the loss of such a loyal, affectionate companion who has provided you with so many happy memories. People who do not have pets often fail to realize what a very important part of our lives these animals fill and what a void is created by their absence. Others are more sympathetic and compassionate. You can be assured, however, that if you have chosen a painless, eternal sleep for your pet by "putting him to sleep" (an appropriate euphemism in this case), you have done him a final service as a loving, considerate friend.

CHAPTER 11

Identification

There are several ways of identifying your dog. The old standby is a collar with dog license, rabies, and ID tags. Unfortunately, collars have a way of being separated from dogs and tags fall off. We're not suggesting you shouldn't use a collar and tags. If they stay intact and on the dog, they are the quickest method of identification.

For several years, owners have been tattooing their dogs. Some tattoos use a number with a registry. Herein lies the problem, because there are several registries to check. If you wish to tattoo your dog,

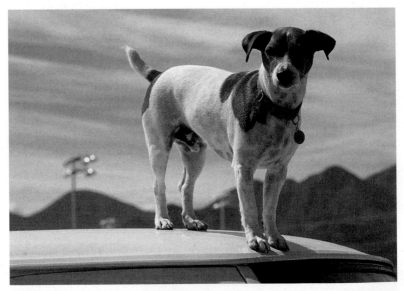

Make sure you have a clear, recent photo of your dog in case he becomes lost.

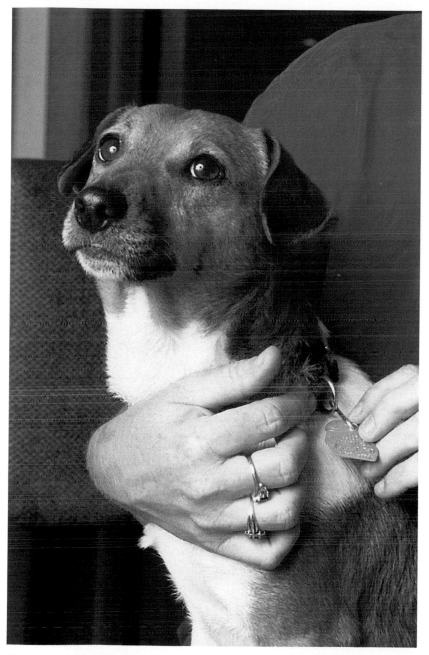

Tattooing and microchipping are great methods of identifying your Jack Russell Terrier if he should ever become lost. Your dog should also wear his collar with his ID tags at all times.

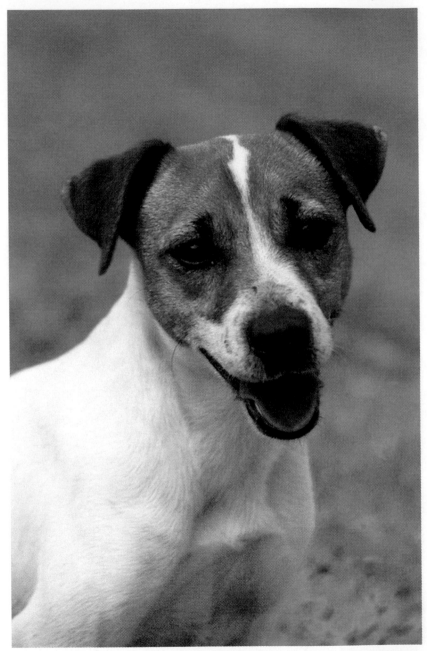

If your Jack Russell Terrier should become lost, contact your neighbors as well as local animal shelters and rescue groups. They can help you locate and retrieve your missing pet.

use your social security number. Humane shelters have the means to trace it. It is usually done on the inside of the rear thigh. The area is first shaved and numbed. There is no pain, although some dogs do not like the buzzing sound. Occasionally, tattooing is not legible and needs to be redone.

The newest method of identification is microchipping. The microchip is a computer chip that is no larger than a grain of rice. The veterinarian implants it by injection between the shoulder blades. The dog feels no discomfort. If he becomes lost and is picked up by the humane society, they can trace you by scanning the microchip, which has its own code. Most microchip scanners are friendly to other brands of microchips and their registries. The microchip comes with a dog tag saying the dog is microchipped. It is the safest way of identifying your dog.

FINDING THE LOST DOG

Most people would agree that there would be little worse than losing your dog. Responsible pet owners rarely lose their dogs. They do not let their dogs run free because they don't want harm to come to

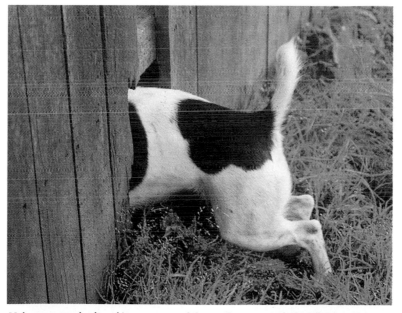

Make sure your backyard is escape-proof if you allow your Jack Russell Terrier free rein in your yard.

them. Not only that, but in most, if not all, states there is a leash law.

Beware of fenced-in yards. They can be a hazard. Dogs find ways to escape either over or under fences. Another fast exit is through the gate that perhaps someone left unlocked.

Below is a list that will hopefully be of help to you if your dog becomes lost. Remember, don't give up, keep looking. Your dog is worth your efforts.

1.   Contact your neighbors, and put flyers with a photo on it in their mailboxes. Information you should include would be the dog's name, breed, sex, color, age, source of identification, when your dog was last seen and where, and your name and phone numbers. It may be helpful to say the dog needs medical care. Offer a reward.

2.   Check all local shelters daily. It is also possible for your dog to be picked up away from home and end up in an out-of-the-way shelter. Check these, too. Go in person. It is not enough to call. Most shelters are limited as to the time they can hold dogs before they are put up for adoption or euthanized. There is the possibility that your dog will not make it to the shelter for several days. He could have been wandering or someone may have tried to keep him.

3.   Notify all local veterinarians. Call and send flyers.

4.   Call your breeder. Frequently, breeders are contacted when one of their breed is found.

5.   Contact the rescue group for your breed.

6.   Contact local schools—children may have seen your dog.

7.   Post flyers at the schools, groceries, gas stations, convenience stores, veterinary clinics, groomers, and any other places that will allow them.

8.   Advertise in the newspaper.

9.   Advertise on the radio.

CHAPTER 12

Traveling With Your Pet

Your dog can be trained to become a very good traveler provided you begin training him when he is still young. Unfortunately, your puppy's first ride in the car is likely to be to the veterinarian's office for his first checkup and shots. So, is it any wonder he doesn't look forward to the jangle of your car keys? This can be avoided, however, with a few, simple tricks.

When traveling with your Jack Russell Terrier, make sure that he is wearing his collar and leash.

TRIPS BY CAR

Familiarize your pet with your car by taking him to a nearby park or open area where he can run around and enjoy himself. Thus, you will have associated the car with something pleasant. When you place his crate on the back seat of the car, throw a dog biscuit or favorite toy into it to preoccupy him. Never allow your dog to ride uncrated, as there is nothing more dangerous than a playful pup jumping on his owner as he is driving. Your puppy should also keep his head inside a moving car because dust and debris could irritate his eyes and nostrils.

Never park your car and leave your pet in it unattended. It takes only a few moments for the heat or cold to become unbearable or deadly to your dog.

LONG TRIPS

When you prepare for a lengthy trip, make certain that you pack a few essential items for your canine companion: a blanket, a thermos of water, pet food, his food and water dishes, favorite toys, and any necessary medicine.

Do not give your pet a heavy meal before the trip, but do ensure that he has a plentiful water supply. This will mean that you will

Your Jack Russell Terrier will be grateful to you for the rest of his life if you take care of him properly when traveling.

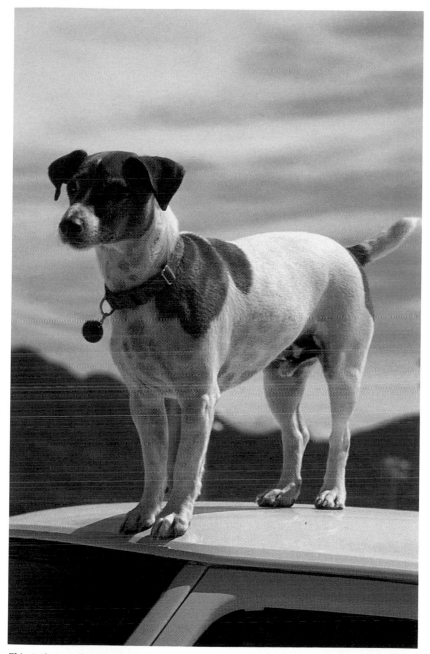

This Jack Russell Terrier loves to travel. A crate is the safest way to transport your dog in the car.

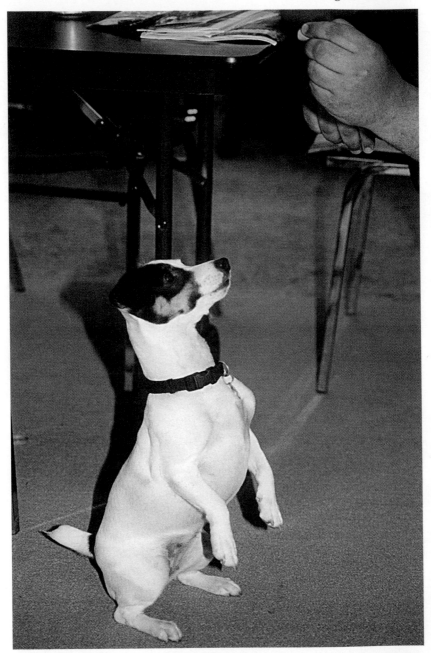

Don't make your Jack Russell Terrier beg to go on trips with you. If possible, take her everywhere that you go.

have to break your journey several times so that he can relieve himself, but the rest stops and exercise will probably do you both good.

Several hotel chains in the United States welcome well-behaved pets, but it is always wise to ask about their policies ahead of time when you make your reservations.

With basic training and a little common sense, you and your pet will make excellent traveling companions and benefit from each other's company along the way.

BOARDING YOUR DOG

It may be necessary to board your dog while you are on an extended vacation or business trip. In this event, there are several courses of action one may take. Ask your vet to recommend a qualified pet sitter or kennel. In the United States, kennels that are members of the American Boarding Kennels Association (ABKA) should provide very good care for your pet. The ABKA is a nationwide nonprofit organization established to promote high standards and professionalism in the pet-boarding industry.

Make certain to visit the kennel for an inspection before you board your dog. Examine the facilities, check the cleanliness of the stalls and exercise runs, talk to the owners about any special dietary or medical requirements your dog may have, look at the dogs staying there, and find out if there is a veterinarian on call. Also, make your reservation well in advance, particularly if you plan to be away in the summer months or during the holidays.

While this may be a stressful time for your dog, you can help your pet feel less homesick by taking his bed or favorite toy along. Finally, remember to leave an address or telephone number where you can be reached in case of an emergency.

Resources

Jack Russell Terrier
Association of America
Corres. Secretary:
Sandy Peterman
RR 2 Box 202
Williamsport, PA 17701

Breeder Contact:
Linda Barden
1 Burns Street
Chicopee, MA 01020
413-533-7224
agiletex@the-spa.com

Rescue:
Jack Russell Terrier
Association of America
Lee Sweitzer
570-265-2606, Pennsylvania
poplarhill@sosbbs.com

American Kennel Club
260 Madison Avenue
New York, NY 10016
or 5580 Centerview Drive
Raleigh, NC 27606
919-233-3600
919-233-9767
www.akc.org

The Kennel Club
1 Clarges Street
Picadilly, London WIY 8AB,
England

Canadian Kennel Club
100-89 Skyway Avenue
Etobicoke, Ontario, Canada
M9W6R4

United Kennel Club, Inc.
100 E. Kilgore Road
Kalamazoo, MI 49002-5584
616-343-9020
www.ukcdogs.com

Index

Index

The Publisher wishes to acknowledge the following owners of the dogs in this book: Jane Bolus; Leroy Chesser; Patricia S. Coe; April Couch; Patricia Crammer; Kit Dorr; Janet Fredericks; Patti Holt; Cynthia L. Hysong; Suellen C. Mally; Kay Monaghan; Michelle Reilly; Kim Richey; Kimberli Romanek; James J. Rushing, DVM; Maria M. Sacco; Mary & John Sweeney; Shirley J. Taylor; & Kenneth Williams.

Photo Credits:
Mary Sweeney—p. 17, p. 22, p. 28, p. 59, p. 63, p. 99, p. 111, p. 131, p. 133, p. 138 & p. 154
All other photos by Isabelle Francais